IAN MORTIMER

WHY
RUNNING
MATTERS

Lessons in Life, Pain and Exhilaration
– From 5K to the Marathon

summersdale

WHY RUNNING MATTERS

An Hachette UK Company
www.hachette.co.uk

Summersdale Publishers Ltd
Part of Octopus Publishing Group Limited
Carmelite House
50 Victoria Embankment
LONDON
EC4Y 0DZ
UK

www.summersdale.com

Printed and bound by CPI Group (UK) Ltd, Croydon, CR0 4YY

ISBN: 978-1-78685-946-4

Substantial discounts on bulk quantities of Summersdale books are available to corporations, professional associations and other organisations. For details contact general enquiries: telephone: +44 (0) 1243 771107 or email: enquiries@summersdale.com.

This book is dedicated to my sons,
Oliver and Alexander Mortimer,
who ran with me throughout 2017
and inspired me to write what follows.

Ian Mortimer is a prize-winning historian and novelist, the author of twenty books, well known for his bestselling *Time Traveller's Guides* to Medieval and Elizabethan England and Restoration Britain. He lives with his wife and family in the small town of Moretonhampstead, in Dartmoor National Park, Devon. Further information about him and his work is available on his website, www.ianmortimer.com.

CONTENTS

AUTHOR'S NOTE
Units of Measurement

Most of the events described in this book are parkruns, which are all 5 kilometres (5K) in length. However, I measure my pace in minutes per *mile*. And that's just the first of a number of complications. There's no avoiding the fact that my generation's use of measurements is a real dog's breakfast. Growing up in the 1970s, our parents talked in terms of feet and inches for height and depth, used yards for longer distances and miles when out walking or driving. But at school we were taught the metric system, and the running races in which we took part on sports day or watched on television were measured in metres. Therefore people of my vintage tend to use millimetres for very small measurements (of the sort you'd normally get in scientific experiments); feet and inches for larger distances (such as someone's height); yards for yet larger ones (such as the length of a cricket pitch); multiples of 100 metres (for those that relate to Olympic track events); and miles for long distances.

Normally a book should standardise on either the metric or the imperial system, but in this case it hasn't been possible. In theory, I could say 'my pace is 5 minutes per kilometre' (rather than 8 minutes per mile) but as I measured all the times at mile-long intervals, telling you my time per kilometre for each distance of 1.609 kilometres would be perverse. As a result, I have made a clear split between the two systems. Apart from the unchangeable distances of events measured in kilometres, such as a 5K parkrun, I employ miles for all distances of half a mile or more and the metric system for anything less.

INTRODUCTION

On 23 April 2017, three hours into the London Marathon, a runner made his last delirious steps towards the finish line. For the last 4 miles he had battled against fatigue; now he had reached the very limit of his endurance. With less than 200 metres to go, in front of the cameras and the huge crowds, he staggered forward, legs awkwardly apart, clearly determined to finish. But he was barely able to stand. Runners swarmed past. He swayed. A fellow competitor stopped and asked him if he was okay. As he did so, the poor man crashed on to his back. Ignoring the chance to continue his own race, the helper lifted the man to his feet. He fell again. So the Good Samaritan picked him up, hauled his arm over his shoulder, and walked with him to the finish line. Next day, the front pages of all the newspapers carried a picture of the two of them. The great story of that race was not who won or how fast the winning time was. For once, no one even cared who had the most extraordinary costume. The headline of *The Times* summed it up perfectly: 'Marathon's true winner is human kindness.'

This scene vividly showed everyone the truth about running. It's not about the *running*. It is about the challenges we face and how we measure up to them. It is about companionship. It is about endurance, ambition, hope, conviction, determination, self-respect and inspiration. It is about how we choose to live our lives, and what it means to share our values with other people.

I had been thinking about this whole phenomenon for a few months before I watched Matthew Rees help David Wyeth over the line that day. For me, the epiphany had been a 5K parkrun with my thirteen-year-old son, Oliver. We had driven into Exeter together, both of us somewhat glum. I had a pain in my hip; he was just in a bad mood. Nevertheless, I managed to set a time I had been trying to run for months. I was exultant – jubilant, even – but where was Oliver? Way back, more than 2 minutes outside his best. When he finished he was despondent and uncommunicative. Asked about his run, he replied simply, 'Awful.' He did not ask about mine, and I hadn't the heart to tell him. He changed out of his running kit and, with a hug and a wistful 'See you later, Dad', headed off into town to do whatever teenage boys get up to when their parents aren't around. I drove home and went back to work. But about 2 hours later I received a telephone call. It was Oliver – the first time he had ever rung me on my office line. He had checked my result as well as his own and knew instantly what that time would mean to me. He was so eager to congratulate me he had to ring straight away, even though he was just about to catch the bus home. As I put the phone down, I reflected on how lucky I was – not because I had achieved my target time but because I had such a son.

You can't experience moments like these and not be aware that people who run together share a bond. They may have many things in common anyway but running together imparts insights, values and understandings that go far beyond their normal level of kinship or friendship. That realisation made me compose a list of all the other things that I had learned from running. As I did so, I found myself writing the following line:

First you run for fitness. Next you run for speed. Then you run for meaning.

For a brief moment I toyed with the idea of beginning a book with those words. Almost immediately, however, my literary inner policeman stepped in. Running is essentially a humble pursuit. It is the very antithesis of such portentous and grandiose phrases. If I were to start with such a mantra, people would undoubtedly shake their heads and reply: 'No, Ian, we just run in our own separate ways for our own individual reasons, don't try to tell us why.' Besides, who would want to read a book about running by me? I'm a historian and novelist by profession, not an athlete; what do I know? I'm not even fast for my age. However, those words did not go away. They lingered in my mind, especially the *you run for meaning* bit.

Five months passed. Gradually I came to realise that if you want to write about running, it's what you have to say that matters, not how fast you run. Let the good runners demonstrate their extraordinary skills in winning races, that is their strength. Mine is writing. One day I remembered that the very first time I'd had to use my literary skills outside a classroom I was similarly unqualified to write about the subject in question. It was when I was at boarding school, aged fourteen. I found that I could avoid the welter of punishments that the senior boys inflicted on us daily by supplying them with erotic fiction. At that age I hadn't attempted a quarter of the sexual shenanigans I wrote about, and many of my peers had much more experience with girls than I did, but I had buckets of imagination and an eye for detail. In this way I managed to avoid punishment totally for a whole year. Reflecting on that experience, I realised there was no excuse for putting off my running book any longer. After all, if you can write about people having fun with their kit *off*, you should certainly be able to describe them doing so with their shorts *on*.

Having thus looked beyond my athletic shortcomings, I felt free to describe what running means to me and the people I know. It poses profound questions, prompting you to consider everything from your self-belief and physical fitness to the choices you make and what it means to be alive. Unlike every other competitive activity I can think of, there are no rules as to how you actually do it – except those which guard against cheating – and yet, partly because of this absence of direction, you cannot help but develop a myriad of mental strategies to enable you to get from A to B as quickly or as comfortably as possible. And that just accounts for how you deal with your *personal* challenges. How you might help other people meet their ambitions adds another mass of intellectual and emotional calculations. This is why every run makes me feel like I am entering a great cathedral for the first time. I am an open-mouthed spectator, looking up, simply amazed at what there is to behold. I see acts of kindness and consideration, even among strangers. I see courage, determination, sadness, resignation and joy in almost every event. Most of all, I see the difference between thinking of myself as an *individual* – someone who is divided off from the crowd – and as a *person*, someone who is connected in some way to everyone else. Given this level of inspiration, it is hardly surprising that I wanted to share my thoughts. If you stumbled into a great cathedral for the first time, would you not want to tell people about it?

I had a second reason for wanting to write about running. I was forty-nine, approaching the half-century bell. Although I could not know how many laps of life's circuit I had left to run, this much was obvious: fifty would mark the beginning of a decade that carried with it the responsibility to prepare for diminishing physical ability and, eventually, death. Fifty might not seem that old these days but in the past, most people would have counted themselves lucky to reach that age. As recently as

1900, life expectancy at birth for British men was forty-four, and for women forty-eight. At the same time, I was aware that it would be morbid to prepare for my twilight years and not celebrate still being alive. Indeed, the very awareness of death's distant drum gave me reason to celebrate life more than ever before. As Nikos Kazantzakis put it in *Zorba the Greek*, 'Leave nothing for death but a burned-out castle.' Why leave your wine cellar stocked with your finest vintages? Why leave any books unwritten, any songs unsung, any sweetness untasted? Leave no race unrun! The man or woman who comes last in a race is at least beating those who do not take part. He or she is at least beating death.

So I decided to write this book. Or, to be precise, at the end of 2016 I made two New Year's resolutions that led to me doing so. The first was to take part in 50 amateur events over the course of the forthcoming year: 45 parkruns and five half marathons. The second was to write down not only what happened during each of those runs but also what I learned in the process. I hoped to produce a book that readers would find thought-provoking, whether they be runners, parkrunners, half-marathoners, aspiring marathon runners – or simply people approaching middle age wondering if running might help them come to terms with watching the years flash by.

I hope I have succeeded. I hope you enjoy the result. But I hope even more that you take something from your running as a consequence of reading this book and use it to your advantage. For while books are often described as 'treasure chests', this one is the key to riches you already have in your possession.

And maybe even to your own great cathedral.

1 | THE JEWEL OF EQUALITY

31 December 2016

As you probably know, parkrun is a weekly 5K run that takes place every Saturday in hundreds of different locations around the world. It was established by Paul Sinton-Hewitt at Bushy Park in West London in October 2004. A second weekly parkrun started up on Wimbledon Common in January 2007, and by the end of that year there were three more: in Banstead, Richmond Park and Leeds. A year later there were 15; a year after that, 35. At the time of writing there are more than 450 parkruns in the UK and over a thousand worldwide. Over 110,000 people in Britain alone run the standard distance of 5K every weekend, supported by some ten thousand volunteers. In Devon, near my home in Moretonhampstead (or 'Moreton', as we call it), there are parkruns at Parke (7 miles away), Exeter (13 miles) and Killerton (20 miles). And from today there is a fourth one, the Torbay Velopark parkrun, 24 miles away. That's where we're going this morning, to the very first event there.

It is still dark when the alarm goes off at 7 a.m. I feel for my running clothes, trying not to disturb my wife, Sophie, who has no wish to spend her Saturday morning struggling around a muddy field with a number of other panting, grimacing people. I find my watch and the wristband with my all-important barcode, get dressed and go to wake the others who are going to run with me. Oliver is already up and about, eating a yoghurt. My two brothers and their families are both staying with us for the festive season, so Oliver and I will be accompanied by my brother, Robbie, and my fifteen-year-old nephew, Tom. My other brother, David, is coming along to support us. On the other hand, my daughter, Elizabeth, is definitely not coming. As far as she's concerned, running is just something that happens to other people. That's okay by me; not everyone loves running. Besides, she has her GCSE exams to revise for this summer, so we have reached an agreement: if she works hard, I won't even ask her to run with us. My eldest son, Alexander, is fast asleep. It was his eighteenth birthday yesterday and we celebrated late into the night. I am still feeling the after-effects myself.

By 8 a.m. we are driving down to Torbay. It is daylight now but the sky is almost the same colour as the road. It seems reluctant to give up its darkness, clinging to the grey like a child clings to a favourite blanket.

Everyone expects me to finish first out of the four of us. I feel my hip, which still has not properly recovered from a stress fracture in early September, and explain that when I last attempted a parkrun, I was almost 2½ minutes outside my best. My brothers both mock me but in truth I am in no shape. An osteopath told me to avoid all weight-bearing exercise for eight weeks. I managed five. It was hard, not running, and feeling myself growing weaker and weaker. *Remember this when you are running and feel you want to stop*, I told myself. *Sometimes it is hard not to run, so appreciate it when you can.*

Almost four hundred of us have turned up for the first Torbay Velopark event. Looking around I recognise a number of faces from other parkruns, including several sub-17:00 runners. I wonder who will come first. After all, a race that no one has previously run is about as equal a competition as there can be. No one has the advantage of knowing the course better than his rivals. But that word 'equality' is a slippery one. We use it with such little thought for what it actually means. And what *does* it mean?

When the whistle goes, the men who can maintain speeds of 5:30 per mile go streaking ahead. Within a minute there is a long string of runners along the first 300 metres of the velopark course. Within 11 minutes the leaders have lapped the tail-enders and are heading out of the velopark into a large field to complete the third and last mile of the run. I watch them across the circuit, gliding around the ground as if tiredness and muscle fatigue mean nothing to them and the only limit on their speed is the length of their stride. I follow at a pace that is more than a minute per mile slower, with all the huffing and puffing gracelessness of someone pushing a shopping trolley over newly ploughed soil. As I complete the second lap of the velopark and head into the field, I find myself slipping on the wet turf, and dodging the deeper puddles. My pace then drops even more and my recent lack of exercise begins to show. After 2½ miles I am practically down to a fast jog. Still, at least my record of outperforming the rest of the family seems to be holding good. But with 100 metres to go, Tom sprints past me, waving and smiling. 'Well done,' I shout. I finish 7 seconds behind him.

So much for equality, you might say. One moment we are all together and have as much of a chance to win as any other man or woman; the next we are anything but equal as our physical build, strength, speed training and stamina all sort us into performance order. As we check in our barcodes – to log our times officially – about a quarter of the field is still running. At what point were we equal? Now? Definitely not. At the start? Hardly. You could say therefore that running reveals our inequality. You could also say that it reminds us that such inequality is natural and unavoidable, and even that this is a good thing. Just think how different it would be if we were all the same fitness and ability, jostling and fighting as we went around the circuit in a tight bunch, getting in each other's way and tripping each other up. But to look at it that way is to see equality as a flat line. One-dimensional. Actually, it's much more interesting than that.

A friend of mine grew up in an underprivileged part of Cornwall but won a place at a grammar school, which introduced him to a middle-class environment. When he went to his new school he discovered that the boys there had the best of everything – the best calculators, clothes, cricket bats, tennis racquets – and they looked down on him. But when it came to running, he did not need any fancy equipment except a good pair of shoes: he could run 800 metres in under 2 minutes. In this way he earned their respect. But what he gained was not equality. He simply replaced one inequality with two others that were more to his advantage: natural talent and determination.

Now consider what happened today. On the strength of Tom sprinting past me you might observe that a forty-nine-year-old writer has no chance against a fifteen-year-old schoolboy who trains with an amateur football club twice a week. However, the second-placed runner today was even older than me – in his early fifties – yet he finished in a time of 17:36. Running isn't as predictable as a simple 'youth beats age' equation. Many other factors come into play, including natural talent; state of health; weight; whether people are running with children; whether they are members of a hard-training running club; whether their jobs leave them free to train midweek; whether they *want* to run fast or have come along merely to meet like-minded people; and how heavily they celebrated their son's eighteenth birthday the night before. With all these points to consider you have to ask what exactly do we mean by 'equality'? Men are generally faster than women. The old aren't equal with the young, the unwell aren't equal with the fully fit, nor the overweight with the lean, and so on. In today's event, participants were only 'equal' in respect of their right to take part, and the fact that it was everyone's first run on this course.

I like this complex situation of a million inequalities all revealing themselves silently along the track. It demonstrates that the concept of 'equality' is a multi-faceted jewel, not just a plain line. You can be 'equal' to everyone else in a particular respect – equal in age, or 'equal in the eyes of the law', or 'equally qualified' – but you can't be equal with everyone else in *every* respect. Think of a pendant diamond, turning slowly in the light: each cut facet reveals another aspect of our equality or inequality with the rest of mankind. What's more, just as you can be equal to someone else in one or two things but not every respect, so it follows that you cannot be *unequal* to someone else in every way. There are many different ways of facing inequality, just as my Cornish friend showed at his grammar school. I find this thought most uplifting. No one is completely unequal or disadvantaged.

Back at home, waiting for the official times to be sent through by email, I read the online newspapers about the national heroes who have been honoured in today's New Year's Honours list. They have all managed to turn one aspect of their lives into world-beating success. And yet the facets of the jewel of equality reflect so many other aspects that are completely ordinary. Suddenly these people seem real. They too face utility bills, government bureaucracy, lovers' tiffs, parking tickets, fear of heights, the common cold, oversleeping and bad dreams. And in that moment,

I glimpse a small truth at the heart of that glinting jewel that is so ordinary that we never give it a second thought.

★ Every single achievement is, in some small way, accomplished in the face of adversity.

2 | A WELL-TAILORED LIFE

7 January 2017

I started this book with two New Year's resolutions: to run forty-five parkruns and five half marathons, and to write about them all. But just *two* resolutions doesn't seem quite ambitious enough for the year in which I turn fifty. So I've added a further forty-eight.

Several of them are about making time for things. For instance, I've resolved to take my wife out to dinner at least once every month; to play a game of chess each week with Oliver; to take my daughter to the cinema at least five times and to work on producing an album of my songs with Alexander (who is studying music production). I've resolved to celebrate my twentieth wedding anniversary and fiftieth birthday in style. I'm planning to play my guitar every day, cook for the family at least once every week, take my kayaks out at least twice over the year, swim in the sea at least once, see a Shakespeare play, see a modern play, organise three concerts by world-renowned musicians, buy at least one original painting by a living artist, read at least one novel and one biography, and so on. On the physical activity front, in addition to the parkruns and half marathons, I've resolved to walk across Dartmoor with my sons (if they will come with me); walk 4 miles every day that I do not run; and do a 4-minute plank and at least 30 press-ups three times a week.

Fifty New Year's resolutions might seem a little excessive, I grant you, though it is an exciting challenge in itself. (Can I do them all? Even half?) But challenge is only part of the explanation. A stronger incentive is my firm belief that we should tailor our lives to fit our personalities and not simply adopt off-the-peg lifestyles, simply doing what everyone else thinks is normal. For example, I do not have a mobile phone. As a result I don't suffer from any of the anxieties that seem to afflict those who are constantly checking their text messages. Similarly, I refuse to use a microwave or fly in an aeroplane. I don't use power-hungry tools if a hand-held equivalent does just as well. This is not an anti-technology stance, but rather a consideration of how we should not lose touch with the reality of things or weaken ourselves through laziness. As for not flying, it is so much better to travel properly, over land, looking at the places we visit. Who really wants to be sucked up in a metal tube and simply injected into a far-flung city?

This tailoring of lifestyle applies to running too. No one accidentally becomes a runner, you have to choose to do it. We select our activities and our targets according to what we want to be. Hence the bond that exists between athletes of all abilities. Our reasons for running might vary but the very choice to run separates us from all of those who choose not to run – and especially from those who do not make lifestyle choices at all.

My resolution to run 45 parkruns and five half marathons adds up to a total of 205 miles. However, in order to have a chance of doing even one half marathon I have to get fit again, and there is no substitute for training runs, which will treble or quadruple that total. The first long race which I've entered is the Bath half marathon on 12 March, just over 2 months away. But I need to start slowly, on account of my hip. So I've chosen a 5-mile run along quiet lanes, which is steep in three places. I am not expecting a fast time. Not only are my muscles weak, I am also carrying an extra stone in weight. I was 13 st 2 lb on New Year's Day – a BMI of exactly 25 – and I've only managed to shed 2 lb of that. Unsurprisingly, my first mile is 40 seconds slower than my best. But when we come to the second steep incline, I am gratified to pass the points at which I used to stop when I was first learning to run up these hills. *Knowing* I can run up such inclines gives me an advantage I did not have first time around. Eventually, with my heart beating as fast as a hummingbird's wings, I reach the top and lengthen my stride back to Moreton. My finish time is nearly 3½ minutes slower than I've run in the past, but it's a start. Every run is part of an improvement process, even if it is not an improvement in itself.

No run is ever wasted.

Oliver and I have chosen Exeter Riverside for the first parkrun of 2017. This is because he is desperate to break

25 minutes, and Exeter is where he ran 25:10 last year. It is completely flat – half on tarmac paths, half around a large playing field – so it is suitable for setting some fast times. At least, it is when it's dry. I look out at the bare trees glistening and dripping in the garden. The grass is sodden. We'll be slipping all over the place. But Oliver is not put off. He is eager for the chance to run.

Almost three hundred of us turn up. Oliver points to the 25-minute pacer, wearing a yellow bib. 'I am not going to let that man out of my sight,' he declares emphatically. True to his word, he even walks to the start line with him. I wish him good luck, and the whistle goes.

Hemmed in at first, it takes me a while to move to the edge of the track, right alongside the edge of the canal. I have visions of falling in. It would be just my luck – and no doubt the local paper would enjoy the story: 'Historian falls in England's oldest canal'. But soon the danger has passed and I am running steadily. It feels quite comfortable, in fact. I look at my watch. No wonder: *I am taking it too easy. I need to speed up.* But I can't. My legs have found their rhythm and just don't respond. At the end, my time is the second-slowest I have ever run on this course.

I turn around to look for Oliver. I walk back, hoping to see him. The 25-minute pacer sprints towards the finish but Oliver is not with him. I remember his exact words, that he 'would not let the man out of his sight'. I eventually find him about 2½ minutes back, soldiering on. As we run in together, with me encouraging him, I think to myself how small a thing it is and yet how poignant. We lose sight of our dreams too easily. And it can be with the best will in the world, when you are working so hard, and striving with such effort. In fact, sometimes the effort itself is what gets in the way. The pain of the run means you lose sight of the man in the 25-minute bib – or of spending time with your family.

That, I realise, is the real reason underlying my 50 New Year's resolutions. I need to do all I can to keep the pacer in sight – the man with the tailored life who not only runs but goes to the cinema with his daughter and still takes his wife out to dinner, plays music and chess with his sons, and goes to the theatre, puts on concerts and buys paintings.

He is the man I really want to be.

3 | THE COMPETITIVENESS SCALE

14 January

This week I have been stuffed with food like a turkey approaching Christmas. It's not just gluttony. I have two books coming out this year: *The Time Traveller's Guide to Restoration Britain*, which appears in April, and a novel, *The Outcasts of Time*, which will be published in June. Meetings over lunches to discuss them with editors, agents and event organisers are important. However, they do nothing for my fitness, especially when they involve travelling to London and hours sitting still on a train. This morning I was once more on the cusp of being overweight.

The reality is that I am going to have to diet seriously if I want to get back to 12 st 4 lb. My strategy involves a series of 'fasting days' and 'diet days', as I call them. On a fasting day I'll consume no more than 360 kcals per 36-hr day (that is a night and a day and the following night). On diet days I limit myself to 600 kcals before 6pm, with no alcohol after that. The regime requires one fasting day and one diet day per week, which for me should result in a sustainable average weight loss of 2½ lb every 7 days. I know I can do it as I've done it before, but the thought of undergoing all that self-denial *again* is depressing. It's a bit like returning from the summit of Mount Everest only to find you've left your car keys at the top.

Oliver won't be running with me today as he is taking part in his first match for the Devon Junior Chess Team. They are playing away, against Wales. I drop him off at the coach stop in Exeter, and then drive down to Parke, a National Trust-owned country house, where my local parkrun takes place.

It is very cold, bright and beautiful, the grass pale green with frost. I jog part of the course in advance. Some sections are icy, others are a quagmire, depending on whether the path is open to the sky or under the cover of trees. The route that forms the first 400 metres is particularly treacherous. Normally visitors run down it in summer and, looking across the parkland, think, *Wow! This is beautiful – the ideal parkrun!* They won't be thinking that today; they'll be too busy watching their step. And then comes the surprise: after that first glorious 400 metres downhill you go through a gate, turn a corner and are confronted with a daunting climb up a 1-in-4 slope. Visiting runners suddenly coming face to face with that quickly revise their opinion of Parke as the 'ideal' parkrun. It is a challenge at the best of times. Today it is slippery with mud and leaves. And further on, the section in the middle is solid ice. I can see the organisers might well decide it is just too dangerous. But rather than cancelling, they decide to mark off a separate route across the frosty grass, to avoid the initial descending path, and to station extra marshals at the frozen midway point to warn people.

Just before the whistle goes, there are several announcements. One of the organisers calls out, 'Is Ian Mortimer here?' I put my hand up. 'Ian is competing in his fiftieth parkrun today,' he declares to the hundred or so assembled runners. They give me a generous round of applause. He adds, 'Ian was so keen to run that although I wanted to cancel the run on account of the ice, he insisted I didn't. So, if you don't enjoy it, blame him.'

Perhaps it is the organiser's good humour, perhaps it is the sun glinting on the frosted grass or just the beauty of the view across the valley, but when the whistle goes, I charge off like a twenty-year-old. Immediately, I am in second place, a yard or so behind an athletic-looking bearded man. What is surprising is that I feel quite comfortable at this speed. I am still in second as we start to climb the 1-in-4 hill. But I have lost the knack of charging straight up a slippery, steep slope. And I have no confidence that I can maintain this speed for any length of time. As soon as you lose confidence, that's it. Four runners pass me, one of them a young woman with a swishing ponytail. I slip on the fallen leaves and mud. Then two more runners go past. By the time I reach the top, I am in eighth. As we splash along the muddy path through the woods, ducking under branches and stumbling on lumps of rock, I lose a couple more places. *It's a run, not a race,* I tell myself, and add for good measure, *You can be happy with a slow time.*

A friend of mine, Anne-Marie, is marshalling at the most dangerously icy point, which we have to pass twice. She shouts encouragement when she first sees me. Her smile is so lovely that she lifts my spirits: I push on hard through the meadow. I put in extra effort on the old railway line too, and stumble up the next slope and on through the woods. I see a long-haired teenager ahead and I run a little faster. I manage to pass him and have a feeling of pride the next time I see Anne-Marie. 'Only half a mile until you're back in the warm,' she calls out. But as we run up the newly laid-out grass path, my energy levels are low. My feet seem to sink into the ground. The long-haired teenager overtakes me. Eventually I finish sixteenth, 3 minutes and 40 seconds behind the chap in first place.

I catch my breath and turn to face those coming in behind me. As I look at them, I think of Oliver. I miss him. It's not the same, running without people to chat to afterwards. It's like seeing a film at the cinema by yourself: you've got no one with whom to talk about it on the way home. 'What did you think of the moment when… Did you see the actor in…' et cetera. It is through discussing such things with others that we make our experiences richer and more meaningful. As I walk back to the car I reflect that it won't be many years before my children leave home and I'll be on my own for every parkrun. One day, it won't be the runners I see coming in behind me, it will be the spaces between them, where once I saw sons.

That evening I pick up Oliver from the chess team's bus. 'Have you had a good day?' I ask.

'Brilliant,' he replies.

'What was the score?'

'I don't know. But we lost. They were really good.'

'Did you win your games?'

'No, I lost all three. But one of them was amazing.'

How like him to be so positive about crushing defeat. I have to applaud his attitude. And it makes me think: sports and games can be all things to all people. It's not that events like today's parkrun are a run *or* a race, it's that they are whatever you want them to be. If you want it to be competitive, it's a race. If, on the other hand, you want it to be a communal jog, then that is all it is, even if some people go haring off, beards and ponytails swaying from side to side. I am sure that some runners way down the field derived more satisfaction from reaching the finishing line than I did from coming sixteenth. Perhaps two or three of them were even happier than the fellow who came first.

Don't get me wrong, it's not that competitiveness doesn't count. It's rather that participation shades into competitiveness in a single smooth scale. And although you might think that it's entirely up to you as to where you place yourself on that scale, it really isn't. Today I tried to raise and then lower the mark at which I would feel my run was a success. But although I didn't do too badly, I didn't feel satisfied. Your true place on the competitiveness scale is not a matter of choice but belief – just as what you think will happen to you after death is not a case of choice but belief. And if you ask me, that is true for what you will regard as success in life generally, not just running.

4 | RECKLESSNESS

21 January

I'd forgotten how mentally draining fasting days are. If you eat nothing from the time you get up, by late afternoon your mind keeps wandering back to food. You acquire a passionate obsession with crisps or peanuts over the course of just a few hours. Thankfully, running can take your mind off both the hunger and the obsession. Thus my weekly fasting days look something like this: I eat nothing from the time I get up, have a mug of black coffee every time I feel hungry, go for a 5-mile walk for lunch and a 4-mile run for tea, and eat a tin of mackerel or sardines and a piece of fruit for supper. I wouldn't recommend this regime to everyone – or anyone, for that matter; we all have to find our own solutions to losing weight – but if you try it, you'll find it has its compensations. The drinks will distract you from the hunger; the exercise will stifle the obsession with food. And the fish and fruit, which are low in calories, will taste divine after the stomach-murdering hunger you've just been through.

This week's parkrun is at Killerton in East Devon. Given that the Old English word 'ton' means 'place', 'Killer-ton' sounds a rather ominous location for a community event. In fact the name is a corruption of 'Kildrington', which probably meant 'the place of the people of Cwldhere' in Old English, a thousand years ago. These days it is owned by the National Trust. The run starts on the hill overlooking the mansion at the heart of the estate, and winds through the woods behind it, circling the gardens full of specimen trees and rare plants, and ending in a field in front of the building. As for slopes, the second half is flat but the first is certainly not: there is one very steep downhill section, which not even a young man would run at full pace, unless he was incredibly reckless.

We arrive in good time and find ourselves amongst the first to line up. We shiver in the freezing air, jogging on the spot, flexing and stretching limbs, keen to get going.

I see Oliver has a new pair of running gloves.

I am envious.

As we wait, my hip still niggles. It's not a significant pain – I can ignore it when walking and running – but every so often it reminds me that I am not fully recovered. I wonder how many other people here are nursing an injury? Probably most of them, one way or another. All of us line up with our quiet stresses and twinges each week. We don't let them show, of course. Such ailments are like the thousand and one troubles we carry with us wherever we go, from school reports to exorbitant bills or trouble with the neighbour's cat repeatedly peeing on the courgette patch. But our smiles on the start line do not mean they are not there.

Oliver and I wish each other good luck and the whistle goes. The fast crowd sprint ahead. I start slowly. Last night I spent ages trying to persuade a friend to run with us. He declined, on the grounds that I would be too competitive. I denied this at the time but now I think to myself, *He's not here. He can't see me. I can be as competitive as I want!* So off I go. And I love it – leaping over the frozen ruts in the path and the rough stones. When I come to the steep downhill section through the wood, I charge down it as fast as an eighteen-year-old, glee across my face, all caution thrown to the wind. I can barely keep my footing. Under the trees, the steep path is muddy and very uneven, so people are being more cautious than usual. I can't see where to put my feet as I hurtle down but, damn it, nothing is going to stop me! I overtake about twenty people in 10 seconds. And then I set up a steady pace for the rest of the run, finishing in a reasonable time.

As we drive home I find myself thinking about charging down that hill. I could not have stopped even if I had wanted to. I was completely out of control – just as reckless as I was in my youth. *Stupid man! You could have fallen and broken a leg.* But I reject such self-correction. Recklessness has its place. The sense of not knowing your limits is a precious thing, for you would never really find out your true potential if you started off in life fully aware of your limitations. You'd never try to exceed them, let alone extend them. Recklessness allows us to forget that there are such things as barriers, so that nothing is impossible. My historical mind shifts to times when reckless young men made all the difference – when wars were fought with swords, and sailors explored the wider world with an incredible hardiness and an even more extraordinary optimism. The virtues of recklessness, I remind myself, include fearlessness and ambition. Imagine climbing the rigging of a sixteenth-century ship in a gale and crawling out along the yard arm to stow a sail in order to avoid the wind tearing it down. Imagine doing it in the dark, with the ship being lifted and dumped in 60-foot waves! In those days England needed the recklessness of its youths. I suppose that in different ways – for example, computer development, soldiering, test-piloting and business innovation – it still does.

What I take from today is the knowledge that I still have a bit of youthful charging spirit. Perhaps a bit of boyishness or girlishness never truly leaves us. Perhaps those people who say they 'still feel seventeen inside' really do retain a bit of their seventeen-year-old selves. After all, people who liked listening to Led Zeppelin in youth don't get to their fiftieth birthdays and suddenly refuse to listen to anything but Beethoven's late string quartets.

Youthfulness does not dissolve completely but instead breaks up, piece by piece, like chunks of ice on the edge of the Arctic ice shelf. Although some parts drift away and melt, others remain. I think that it is a blessing to retain shards of your youth, in some form or other. And having a little bit of recklessness is no exception to that rule. It means that a part of you truly believes that anything is possible.

5 | IT'S ABOUT TIME

28 January

Oliver and I drive to the beautiful Plym Valley, near Plymouth, on the other side of Dartmoor. We park in an overgrown quarry overhung by trees and ivy, and cross a narrow granite packhorse bridge over the River Plym. The branches above us carry thousands of raindrops on their twigs: these sparkle in the early morning sun, giving the appearance of sheets of delicate brown lace woven with jewels. One man tells us he saw a kingfisher by the path half an hour ago. The ground, however, is so wet that we won't be able to do the usual route through the meadow. Instead we will have to run along the canal towpath, run up onto the disused railway line, come back to a point near the start and then do the whole route again.

The canal. The railway. Although the heavily wooded valley seems natural today those two features remind me that this was once a place of industry. It makes me smile to think that the people who built the canal and the railway in the nineteenth century would have considered their constructions the epitome of progress. They could not possibly have imagined that, less than 200 years later, the railway would be just a leaf-strewn track and two hundred of us would be gathering here to conduct 'a footrace', as they would have called it. For the railway builders, the future was all about *not* having to do things on foot but being transported quickly and cheaply in trains.

Looking at the old railway bridge, I ask myself the question, *why* did people not run as we do today?

You might respond to that by saying, 'You are asking the wrong question, Dr Mortimer; people *did* run. They always have done. Just remember the original Olympic Games, which started in the year 776 BC. Homer's *Iliad* is even older, and that includes many references to running, not least Achilles, "the swiftest of the swift", "swift Ajax", and "swift Aeneas". And then of course you have the story of Pheidippides.'

In case you don't know, Pheidippides was an Athenian messenger. In the year 490 BC he ran 150 miles from Athens to Sparta carrying the Athenians' desperate request for military assistance against the Persians, whose massive fleet was just off the coast. When he arrived, after running for a day and a half, the Spartans said that they were rather busy right now, and the Moon was in an unpropitious phase; please could the Athenians hang on for a few days? Pheidippides ran back to Athens with this disappointing news – only to find the Athenian commanders had left the city with the army to face their grim fate. They had marched out to meet the Persians at Marathon, approximately 26 miles away. So Pheidippides ran to Marathon. When he arrived, he saw Persian bodies strewn all over the beach. Despite being hugely outnumbered, his people had won an incredible victory, so he turned around and ran back to Athens with the news. 'Joy! We've won,' he shouted as he arrived before the Athenian magistrates, whereupon he collapsed and died. Given that he had just run more than 350 miles in 4 days, I'm not entirely surprised.

So, yes, people have run since ancient times. However, they have not always done so in the same way as us, or for the same reasons. The men at the ancient Olympics ran naked, covered in olive oil. They also wrestled naked, boxed naked and jumped naked – hence our word 'gymnasium', which comes from *gymnos*, the Ancient Greek word for 'naked'. As for the *Iliad*, this does include races between the champion runners in the Greek army, but they were warriors. Pheidippides similarly ran because his homeland faced the threat of destruction. Heavens, that was when running *really* mattered! The difference between Pheidippides and today's motley crew of parkrunners at Plym Valley could not be greater: I'm glad our nation's security doesn't depend on any of us running 350 miles in 4 days. Mind you, the thought of everyone here stripping naked and covering themselves in olive oil would probably cause any invading Persians to turn around and head straight back out to sea.

So when did people start to run as a matter of choice?

No doubt the answer to that question differs around the world. The Tarahumara – the long-distance running tribe who were the subject of Christopher McDougall's 2009 book *Born to Run* – have apparently been running for centuries. In England, however, the history of running does not much pre-date the seventeenth century. Smock races, in which young ladies ran for prizes, were held in many places. But these had a specific purpose: drawing crowds to watch the girls showing off their legs and sometimes their breasts. An enterprising chap called Robert Dover started his own annual Olympic Games near Chipping Camden in 1612; these continued on and off until the nineteenth century but were never anything more than a local amusement. Sometimes races were held between noblemen's servants, such as that between a chap called Crow and Lord Claypole's footman in August 1660. Samuel Pepys watched them run three times around Hyde Park: Crow won by more than 2 miles. But here again, these races had an ulterior motive. Betting on a footrace was the next best thing to betting on the horses. It wasn't about the race, it was about the gambling.

Everything started to change with the ability to measure time accurately. Clocks and watches did not have minute hands until about 1680, let alone second hands. Thomas Tompion made a few remarkable watches that measured seconds in the early 1680s but such refined timepieces remained very costly and rare, and only came to be used for measuring runners' times when a wealthy gentleman wanted to have a bet that someone could not run a certain distance in a given time. In 1733 a man called Pinwire apparently ran 10 miles in 52:03. On 9 May 1770 James Parrot won a bet of 15 guineas (£15 15s, the equivalent of a labourer's annual salary) by running a mile in under 4 minutes. And in 1796 a man called Weller reputedly ran a mile in 3:58, again for a bet.[1] While these extremely fast times for the mile are questionable, the important point to note is that people had started to time runners by 1800. The motive was still a wager, but timed runs were becoming more common.

The earliest reference to a 'stopwatch' in the *Oxford English Dictionary* is dated 1740. Nevertheless, stopwatches weren't at all common in the eighteenth century. Only in the 1840s with the development of the 'chronograph' – a watch that recorded intervals of time, which could be reset easily – did the timing of runners become common. In 1855 Charles Westhall ran a mile in 4:28, which was then considered the fastest time ever (people had forgotten about the earlier wagers of a mile in 4 minutes). By 1860 the word 'record' had acquired the meaning of 'the best officially recorded achievement of a particular kind in a competitive sport'. So, while running in general dates back to before the time of the Ancient Greeks, the idea of running against the clock only dates back to the eighteenth century, and the practice of people habitually timing races only goes back to the mid-nineteenth.

A large part of the fun of running together is to see how your times compare with those of other people and with your past runs. How many runners these days *don't* time themselves? Not many. How many people would do a parkrun if there were no times recorded? Many fewer than currently turn out each Saturday. Most of us need to know how fast we have run in order to see how we stand in relation to each other, and to gauge how our performances are progressing (or not).

Today's parkrun is a good example. After the run director blows his whistle, we all charge off up the path beside the canal. About half a mile later, I climb the hill for the first time along with a chap who is about the same age as me. Over the next 2½ miles he and I have an almighty tussle for twenty-fifth place. I eventually force him to settle for twenty-sixth but, as we are so far behind the leaders, I have no idea how good this performance is. What makes every run significant, therefore, is the fact there is a time at the end of it. You need that detail to understand your effort. Today my time was 23:29, a few seconds faster than my previous best. Oliver's time also marked an improvement.

Without a timing system you cannot work these things out. You cannot compete against yourself. Most people can recall exactly what their personal best is at their local track, and some people remember their best at every course they have ever run. To run a fast time is therefore like gaining a new qualification: once you've got it, you will always have it. When I am old and grey I won't be able to run 5K in 23 minutes but nothing can take away from the fact that in Exeter last year I ran the distance in 19:47. A time is thus a form of emotional income. It may well be the reason why you run in the first place – for that great satisfaction of achieving a target time. But unlike a financial income, which you can spend, you can never exhaust an emotional one, no matter how often you 'spend' it. Psychologically, it can enrich you forever.

6 | UNIQUENESS

4 February

There is a monthly folk music night in one of the pubs in Moreton, founded by my good friend Andy Gardner. How should I describe Andy? One way would be to say that, having missed his true vocation as a buccaneer by about three hundred years, he is a carpenter by day, a folk singer after supper, and a ladies' man by night. Another way would be to say that he was the inspiration for the character of Raw Carew, the indomitable pirate in my novel, *The Roots of Betrayal*. Anyway, last Monday was the tenth anniversary of 'folk night'. I had a few pints with him and some mutual friends, and did a bit of singing. Then we hit the whisky. When I finally woke up, I had lost count of the number of drinks I'd had. All I could remember was that Andy had promised to do a parkrun with me at some point before the end of the year. That was the one bit of sanity I was able to salvage from the evening, and I clutched it as tightly as a shipwrecked sailor clings to a piece of driftwood.

This sort of behaviour, as you can appreciate, is not good for your running. It is not good for your fasting either. In short, nothing saps the resolve like alcohol – all your firm promises dissolve in its liquid forgiveness. But, dammit, I'd also eaten like a horse that evening, so the next day simply *had* to be a fasting day. A walk and a run were the only things on the menu. My stomach felt like I was cheating on it – as if my mouth was having an affair with someone else's stomach – but I was resolute. On top of the hunger and hangover, the rain depressed me: it hit me hard in the face, blown by the wind coming across the moor. Then it turned to sleet. And as if that were not enough, for about 2 minutes there was hail.

The heavy rain continued all week. By Friday, the roads were flooded. This part of Devon is like that. The clouds float across Dartmoor, groaning with weight. Like bombers returning from an air raid, they empty themselves of their heavy loads here before drifting over the rest of England, as innocent as cotton wool. Yesterday evening Oliver and I looked at the puddles and discussed our options. There would not be much point in going to any of the flat runs: they would probably be cancelled. Instead, we would have to run somewhere hilly and wooded, like Parke.

As we drive down the road to Parke, with the sun shining on the frosted hills, I think to myself that I must be mad to be doing this. What was Einstein's definition of madness? Doing the same thing repeatedly and expecting to get different results. Here I am, driving down the same old road to the same old place – with yet another hangover – and expecting the results to be different. Einstein would not be proud of me.

Hold on, Einstein. Can we ever do the same thing more than once?

A few years ago, when writing my second *Time Traveller's Guide*, I was suddenly struck by the realisation that every act of seeing is unique. It doesn't matter if you are standing side by side with another person looking at the same view, you are actually occupying two different places and your perspective is slightly different from that of your companion. If you stand in the same spot, your appreciation of the view is obtained at different times: again, one of you might see something the other could not. The differences might be small but that is not the point: *every* act of seeing is unique. And once you appreciate that, then you start to understand that every breath you take is unique too. And every use of every word in the English language has a different context, and thus has a unique significance. The same point applies to running – every run is unique – and not just the physical act, all the things you associate with running and all the thoughts you have as you pace along are similarly unique. Thus you cannot do the same thing twice, not even the same run. The world seems suddenly a richer place when you think of 7 billion people seeing, breathing, running and thinking all independently, in ways never to be exactly repeated in all the future history of the world, like the unique and never-repeating shapes of waves crashing through the centuries on our shores.

My next thought, however, contradicts this. The fact that every wave is different does not mean that they are unalike. In fact, you'd have to be pretty sad to spend your life concentrating on the differences between waves and not the similarities. Likewise, most runs are alike. Occasionally someone will put in an astounding performance but if the same line-up from last week's run were to run again, our times would be more or less the same. Those who ran it in 20 minutes would still beat those whose best is 25. There would be small differences in the positions but overall, the variations would be minimal. Our infinite differences do not imply unpredictability. This is why we can learn from history, even though history never actually repeats itself.

The whistle blows and we are off. I start jogging along in about fifteenth place, dragging my hangover as if it is a ball and chain attached to the inside of my skull. Down the long uneven slope we go, through some huge puddles, and then up the 1-in-4 hill. I charge up it as fast as I can, and get about halfway before I feel the yank of the hangover on its chain and I wonder why I am bothering. Pride forces me on, hauling me forward as the hangover tries to hold me back. At the top, a massive tree that blew down last night lies sawn up on either side of the path; we run across the soaked sawdust, trampling it into the mud. I duck under low branches and swerve to avoid the reaching arms of brambles, whose thorns are particularly brittle and sharp in the cold. A woman with long brown hair passes me. Her running tights show off her figure so alluringly that

I am completely distracted from my bramble-dodging. My hangover clearly thinks the same way for suddenly it pulls me forward and urges me to jog along behind her. However, about a mile further on, she approaches a steep downward slope with caution and I overtake her, my hangover wistfully looking back over my shoulder.

I splash through another muddy puddle, still thinking about uniqueness. My mind shifts to a local planning application for a new industrial building on the site of an old barn in Moreton. I don't want it to be built because of this very point of unrepeatable uniqueness versus predictable ordinariness. The proposers say they want to 'tidy up' the area but what they are proposing is a substantial new industrial building that will give the place the appearance of a business park – something wholly inappropriate for the outskirts of an old moorland town. To my mind, in a National Park, structures that are characterful and unique should always take precedence over standardised and ordinary replacements. If the old barn has to be replaced, let it be rebuilt on the same site in timber and slate. There is no reason why Moreton should not be graced with attractive buildings that reflect its special qualities. Utilitarian architecture is a crime against the spirit of a community.

I must have let my pace fall, for the woman with the alluring tights overtakes me again. I try to follow her but she has paced herself better than me. She pulls away as we run along the old railway line. I canter home well behind her, then jog back down the field and encourage Oliver over the last quarter mile.

Driving away, I reflect on how modern society wants us to behave as standardised units of humanity. Units of educational achievement. Units of employment. It feels as if our environment too is subject to this general will. A school must look like this, an industrial building like that. Great clouds of conformity have settled on the towns and cities of the modern world, and they are having an impact on our villages and hamlets too. I wonder if it was a desire to see everything as unique, homemade and special that made me turn to history, and try to reconstruct a vision of my country before the Industrial Revolution? I don't know about that. But I do know that you can find vestiges of uniqueness in the modern world. You simply have to search for them. Today's run will never be repeated. To the external eye, it might appear just the same as so many other runs here, but if you put in the effort you will remember the sawn-up tree, the woman in the alluring tights, and my thoughts on the arguments about planning permission. Uniqueness is not an absolute: it is a matter of perspective. If you want the world to be composed of rare and unique things, then that is exactly how it is. You just have to make the effort to see it that way.

7 | EXTRAORDINARY PEOPLE

11 February

A lunchtime run was all the nutrition I allowed myself on my fasting day this week. But it amounted to a three-course feast. For the hors d'oeuvres, there was a bitterly cold wind blowing across the moor as I struggled around the first 2.2-mile lap of the summit of Mardon, the largest hill overlooking Moreton. The wind chill factor made 3 degrees feel like minus 3. Then, for the main course, I was treated to a special dish of freezing rain, with the piquant addition of some finely grated sleet. As I hauled my way around four more laps, I splashed through a few side dishes of icy puddles too. Rather than put me off, however, they made me all the more determined to clear my plate. I thought, *okay, let's push on for the whole half marathon. I'm not stopping for puddles, hills, hunger, hail, sleet, rain, cold – nothing.* It was the first time since October I'd attempted to run more than 8 miles, and thus it was not surprising that chafed and bloody nipples and a sore scrotum were on the menu for the third course. But the end was so sweet. I'd covered 13.15 miles and felt no pain in my hip. I was pleased.

On Wednesday evening one of my publishers asked me to come to London to attend a media dinner. I think they were trying to fatten me up as they held it in the private dining room at Fortnum and Mason, the great food store on Piccadilly. Several of the other writers there dealt with matters of great gravity. One, a professor of surgery at UCL, who had previously worked for NASA and international emergency rescue teams, had written a book about decision-making in urgent situations. He talked about looking down from an emergency helicopter on the wreckage of forty or fifty cars on a motorway, and having to decide how to maximise the chances of saving lives. Another speaker, an economist who had served as the Greek minister of finance, spoke eloquently about the problems dealing with the bureaucrats of Europe. The most memorable conversation I had, however, was not with a fellow author but with a TV producer. She used to be a criminal defence barrister but gave it up after two years. I asked her why. 'It is very difficult to deal with the constant pressure of knowing that, if you make a mistake, your client might go to prison for ten years for a crime he didn't commit.'

The following day, on the train back to Devon, I thought about all these high-stakes occupations. Running is the very opposite. What is the very worst that can happen? That you will injure yourself or give yourself a heart attack through overexertion. What's more, running takes your mind off things. If you're a police officer, or a firefighter like my brother Robbie, the professional risks you deal with every day are set to one side when you run. Come to think of it, even a family holiday is more stressful than a run. Running might be hard work physically but, mentally, it is the ultimate escape from pressure.

———————

It is the 300th parkrun at Killerton today. But that is not why we're running here. The real reason is a woman called Maggie Hunt. This is her local parkrun, and I hope to meet her. My wish is granted about one mile into the run. I sense someone coming up behind me and glance over my shoulder to see her there, wearing the distinctive green '250' shirt that denotes the fact that she has completed 250 parkruns. I hear her say some words of encouragement to another woman running with her. I stay at the same pace for most of the second mile. Then at a wide section of path, I decide to put on some speed. I know from last time that my feet will just sink into the soft ground towards the end, whereas the lighter-framed women will glide over it. I finish in a time of 22:02. Maggie comes in 4 seconds behind me.

This is no mean achievement. She is 10 years older than me.

When we survey the full results, I am impressed that five of the top ten finishers are my age classification: 'Veteran Men, 45–49'. I'm impressed by their age grades too. An age grade is the percentage of your speed compared with the world record pace over that distance for someone of the same age and sex. So, for a forty-nine-year-old man like me, world-record pace over 5K is calculated as 14:38 and for a fourteen-year-old boy like Oliver, 14:11. The first of these forty-something men has notched up an age grade of 77.91 per cent, the second 78.25 per cent, and the others are between 70.1 per cent and 72.5 per cent. Mine is a much more humble 66.4 per cent. These percentages do not take into consideration the lie of the land. You can't start altering world-record pace for awkward tree roots, mud, slopes, large stones, awkward sharp turns between gates, and so on. However, the system does allow you to say that the 78.25 per cent effort by the older second-placed runner was an even greater achievement than the winner's 77.91 per cent. It also allows men and women of varying ages to compare their performances.

I might have pipped Maggie for twenty-third place but in truth there was no competition. Her age grade today was 84.16 per cent. This is her 246th run on this course and she has achieved an age grade of 80 per cent or higher on more than two hundred occasions. Her best is over 90 per cent, despite the mud, twists, turns, rocks and slopes; only one person has ever achieved a higher percentage here. Every single week, in age-related terms, she comes first – normally by a very long way. When the current course record was set by a chap in his late twenties in the summer of 2013, his age grading was 83.86 per cent – less than Maggie's today. This run was not even amongst her best hundred performances at this course. She is remarkable. And yet here she is, happily running around the grounds of Killerton week after week, passing on words of encouragement. I find her inspirational.

There are extraordinary people like Maggie to be found in all sorts of places. The landlady at your local pub might be a brilliant musician. The woman who works in the local supermarket might be a gifted linguist, working her way around the world. I think of my brother Robbie whose day job involves saving people from burning buildings and cutting people out of cars quickly enough to get them to intensive care, and lifting up Tube trains after people have fallen underneath the wheels. (Parkrun gently reminds us that many of the people with whom we rub shoulders on a daily basis are truly remarkable. You don't need to be wined and dined at Fortnum and Mason by your publisher to meet them.)

8 | NUMBERS

18 February

I like numbers. They are the most perfect words. When your partner uses the word 'love', you don't know exactly what he or she means, even if you have been married for years. But you know precisely what he or she means by the word 'seven'. I grant you that numbers have their limitations; it is very difficult to tell someone you love them in numbers ('Darling, I love you seven times as much as I love the cat and thirty-three times as much as the washing machine...') However, when you want to prove something, invariably you will have to reduce it to numbers. In this way we reassure ourselves that we know something for certain.

This power of numbers struck me forcibly last year when writing about the seventeenth century. In the early 1600s people's view of the physical world was still wrapped up in religion. They believed in witchcraft and superstition; they sought scientific explanations from bishops and the Pope. If a major conflagration burned down a house or a town, it was an act of God. But then things changed. Dozens of calculators, clocks and measuring devices were invented. The Royal Society was founded. Isaac Newton published *Principia Mathematica* – the mathematical basis of modern science – and fire insurance companies started charging premiums for protecting your house at about the same time. Previously your best defence against the losses incurred by fire had been prayer; by 1700 it was a carefully calculated insurance premium. There is no doubt that our more sophisticated use of numbers changed the world. It's not just the technological changes they allowed. Just think, if you go to buy a sports car and ask, 'How fast will it go?' and the vendor replies, 'Fast', you'd say, 'Yes, but how many miles per hour?' We feel we understand something more completely when we can quantify it.

Armed with precise times, therefore, we can start to look at our runs with a degree of discernment. Consider my last seven parkruns, which were conducted in a wide variety of conditions, across different courses and with varying numbers of runners. Torbay and last week's Killerton run were almost identical times (22:03 and 22:02) but the former course was flat, two-thirds of it on tarmac, and the latter was very uneven. Thus Killerton was a far stronger achievement. Confirmation lies in the much smaller proportion of the field that was faster than me at Killerton (7.8 per cent) compared to Torbay (13.2 per cent). By this reckoning, last week's run was by far my best so far this year.

So how will today compare?

Alexander is joining us. We set off in thick fog. With visibility down to about 30 feet, I drive very slowly into

Exeter. But here and there I notice flowers in the hedgerows, the first signs of spring. We talk about the run ahead. Oliver says he is determined to do three things: 1. beat his older brother; 2. run a personal best; and 3. run under 25 minutes. Alexander doesn't want his fourteen-year-old brother overtaking him, of course. But his heart is not in the running. As we wait for the start, he points to the bright yellow FINISH sign. 'I love that sign,' he says, gazing at it longingly. 'When I next see it, I'll want to kiss it.'

As soon as the whistle goes I know it's not going to be my day.

My legs feel sluggish.

What an appropriate word that is, *sluggish*. I feel like a slug, a sluggard, a slogger. Whatever ancient root lies underneath those words, you know it means something very slow. And I am. Was it the second portion of last night's fish pie, I wonder? Who knows. By the quarter-way mark, I'm almost half a minute down on my best. I persevere on the path through the woods. A dozen people overtake me. Leaving the woods, I can see the leader is already about three-quarters of a mile ahead. But I tell myself: *no run is ever wasted* and think in terms of this just being another small stage in building up my strength. More people overtake me. Back on the bridge with three-quarters of a mile to go, I glance at my watch again: I am almost 2 minutes down on my best. *Damn it, Ian! Use whatever you've got left. Just make sure you beat your last time.*

The result is not a disaster. In amateur running, it never is.

Immediately I run back to find my sons. Oliver is loping along, never speeding up or slowing down. His big brother is about 20 seconds behind him. I shout encouragement to Oliver and urge him on. I glance at my watch. It's going to be very close, whether he makes the 25-minute mark. Then Alexander – all 6 foot 5 inches of him – starts speeding up. 'Push, Oliver, run harder! He's catching you!' I shout. But Oliver's legs obviously don't want to listen: he simply carries on at his usual pace. He keeps going just fast enough to hold his older brother at bay.

'I did not enjoy that one little bit,' exclaims Oliver as the three of us share a hug.

'It's not about enjoyment, it's about satisfaction,' I say.

'Okay, I'm not satisfied either.'

'But you beat me,' says Alexander, sportingly.

'I reckon you might have fulfilled all three of your day's ambitions,' I say. 'You definitely beat your brother, you finished in about twenty-five minutes, and thus you might have run a personal best.'

'Doubt it,' replies Oliver.

Back home, Oliver is in the shower when the results come through. I shout through the door: 'Do you want the good news or the bad news?'

'Both,' he replies.

'The good news is that it was a PB.'

'What's the bad news?'

'25:03.'

'That's not bad news,' he replies. 'I almost did it.'

Bless him.

As I go back downstairs to my study, I reflect on the run. For me it was perfunctory: a time of 21:36. My body just did not want to go to its maximum or anywhere near it. It was not enjoyable and, to tell the truth, Oliver was right: it was not satisfying either. But there were highlights. I was delighted to see the competition between the two boys as they neared the end. I found the good humour in which they raced a joy to witness, and Alexander's sporting comment was admirable. The spontaneous hug with both of them at the end was something to remember.

Yes, today was a good day. It was a day spent with my sons, as we saw the first signs of spring, and everything was right with the world.

Sometimes you know things for certain without any need for numbers at all.

9 | DOES IT MATTER?

25 February

Alexander, Oliver and I are setting out on a bleak, blustery day to Torbay Velopark. Alexander's girlfriend, Sol (short for 'Soleil'), is coming with us, to take photographs. Why? Surely the world does not need pictures of us floundering around in the mud? The answer is that I had a brainwave last week. I had the covers to my next two books printed on some running shirts. On the front is the cover to *The Time Traveller's Guide to Restoration Britain*; on the back is the cover to *The Outcasts of Time*. I'm planning to use her pictures on my website and social media. Even if people don't talk to me about the books, they might register the covers. I plan to run in them for the rest of the year.

I start off reasonably well, completing the first 2 miles in just over 13 minutes, but then we enter the field and the ground becomes very slippery. I struggle to finish in 21:51, which gives me twenty-third place. Alexander just manages to hold off Oliver: they finish in sixty-fourth and sixty-fifth. And frustratingly for Oliver, he is once more a few seconds outside 25 minutes. So no one is particularly happy with his performance when we go for breakfast afterwards. Not until I get home and see that less than 10 per cent of the field was faster than me do I feel good about today's run.

But so what? Does any of this matter?

In the great scheme of things, no, of course, it doesn't matter. With the news on the radio being about the war in Syria, the plight of millions of refugees, the Iraqi army's attack on Mosul, Donald Trump's attempts to control the world's media by labelling as 'fake news' anything that he does not like to hear – with all this going on, then heavens, no, our running doesn't add up to a hill of beans. In fact, it doesn't even constitute a single bean. However, by that reckoning, nothing we do matters very much. It doesn't matter who wins the British Grand Prix, the Ashes or the World Cup. Even the Wimbledon Championships don't matter. But why think this way? It seems to me that the question 'does it matter?' has its roots in the deepest cynicism. It's like the weary 'What's the point?' remark of an idle schoolboy who doesn't want to run on sports day – except that it is turned on you, so you have to justify what *you* do, because he can't be bothered even to work out the reason for himself.

Thoughtful runners will almost certainly sit down at some point and ask themselves why running a faster time *does* matter so much. Why are so many hundreds of thousands of people keen to set a new personal best? Why is Oliver so determined to break the 25-minute barrier? After all, unless you're a world-class athlete, running a fast 5K time is not as significant as getting good exam results, which might affect the rest of your life. Why push yourself to the point of pain for the sake of a few seconds? Is the 'emotional income' really that great? Are not all our times simply 'writ in water', as the romantic poet John Keats said of his own name?

Everyone will come up with their own answer to that, of course, but I imagine that there will be quite a lot of common ground. For example, it's quite clear that there is a whole virtuous circle underlying the desire to run faster. It is much more than simply trying to impress people. But let's start off with that point. It *is* impressive that some people can run fast. When I see amateurs run 5K in under 16 minutes, I am amazed. My best-ever age grade is 73.38 per cent, which suggests that I might have been able to run 17:35 in my late twenties. So anything under 16 minutes is far faster than I could ever have dreamed of running. Nowadays, I want to be the fifty-year-old who can cover the distance in 20 minutes or so. It's part of the tailoring of one's life that I talked about in chapter two. It is a matter of self-respect.

'Self-respect' in this sense goes beyond what I think of myself. It relates to what others think of me too. Through running faster we earn the right to give kudos to others. Think of it in non-running terms. If someone says they enjoy reading my books, that's great. If the person who tells me this is a fellow historian or a bestselling novelist, that's even better. It carries greater weight. The same things go for runners. If I tell a great runner I admire him, it might mean little to him, but if I can run a bit myself, it probably means that much more. If I had taken part in the same race, then it would mean that much more again. And the fact that my admiration is appreciated more would lead in turn to greater self-respect on my part. So you could say that we want to run faster not just to impress other people but also because other people impress us and we want to show that we respect them for their achievements. All our efforts feed into a mutual appreciation of each other's successes – a virtuous circle wherein, by doing well, we inspire others to do just as well, who in turn encourage us to do even better.

This is why performance matters – because we want to maintain the virtuous circle of running, including the shared values and the physical and psychological benefits that measurable improvement brings. The trouble is that, if someone has to ask, 'Does it matter?' in the first place, he or she probably is not going to understand the answer. The real question, therefore, which has much more resonance among those who run, is not whether performance matters but how much? Is running a personal best this week as important to you as attending your child's school play or remembering your wedding anniversary? Probably not. However, in the context of wider society – in the context of the country being at war in the Middle East, say – these too are trivial matters. The point is that seemingly inconsequential things can be hugely important to people. The setting of targets and the fulfilment of ambitions, however small, are the very building blocks of our self-respect and our mutual respect –

and just think what society would be like if we had neither of those.

In fact, that's a really interesting thought. What would the world be like if we had no self-respect?

I reckon it would be sheer anarchy.

10 | IRREPRESSIBILITY

4 March

There are buds in the garden, wild daffodils in the flowerbeds, and primroses in the hedgerows. The air has a freshness that is just a joy to taste. It's like a wonderful flavour that you had always suspected would exist but had never previously found.

But I don't want to run. Not today.

There are several reasons why I do put on my running kit. One is that I resolved to do 45 parkruns this year – and letting this one slip will mean other occasions when I have to run when I don't want to. Another is that I need to keep up my fitness. But the third and most important reason is Oliver. I knock on his door, open it and ask, 'Are you up for a parkrun this morning?' He sits up, blinks, says, 'yes', and gets out of bed straight away. The decision isn't mine to make. It was made long ago, when we recognised running was not just an activity; it was a bond between us.

At Parke, Oliver jogs up and down, warming up, while I chat to a few people. Only about a hundred runners are here, despite the beauty of the sun on the parkland setting. I start at the back, telling myself that I don't need to go fast today. I can just jog around with the crowd. But after the whistle goes, I find those in front of me are running far too slowly, so I overtake them. Now, moving faster, more people seem to be in my way, so I've no choice but to overtake them too. I splash straight through the puddles and muddy patches that others try to skirt around. Clods of earth and drips of muddy water go flying all around us. When I come to the bottom of the 1-in-4 hill, some people start to walk. No! That's not the spirit! I aim for the hard clay-like ground on the right-hand side of the path and charge up it impatiently. Thus I overtake a few more people. That effort leaves me panting and I decide to take it easy. *Now* I can just jog around. But there is a girl ahead who is slowing up, and, if I don't overtake her soon, I'm going to be trapped behind her in a narrow section of the course between the trees. So I run faster again. Not until the first mile is complete do I slow to a steady pace. I know my time will still be poor – it's so muddy everyone will be at least a minute down on their best – but I cannot resist the temptation to pass people when they are running slowly.

Reflecting on the morning, what strikes me most was my lack of choice. I could not have backed out of running. The bond with my son made sure of that. And once there, I did not have much control over how fast I went. I'd have had to go against my instincts in order to run slowly. In such situations our personalities take over and drive us forward or hold us back. We cannot help ourselves.

How much of life is like this, guided by force of character rather than choice? I know philosophers talk at length about free will, and I know there is a wide range of opinion about how much free will we have. However, this practical aspect of decision-making is slightly different. Had you made it a test of my willpower whether I could run very slowly, I would have done so. But that was not the challenge. Doing as well as I could in the circumstances was. And I responded.

I suppose that what this adds up to is not a matter of free will but whether running is an expression of personality or a suppression of it. Haruki Murakami wrote in *What I Talk About When I Talk About Running* that he sometimes runs to think nothing – for the 'void', as he puts it. Not long ago I myself wrote about how running lifts the pressures from your shoulders. But as we all know, when you stop running, the responsibilities are still there. And however much Murakami feels he is in a void, he is still part of the real world. I think that that relief from pressure – the 'void' – does not allow you to lose your character in your surroundings but to become more yourself. When running, our personalities come even more to the fore, without us even realising it. That might find expression in our competitive instincts taking over, or the kindness of one runner stopping to help another, or simply in being so bloody-minded we will never give in. Yes, running brings out the essential parts of our character. And writing those words makes me ask, when am I most myself? When running? Thinking about it, I am most myself when talking or writing about history, playing music, walking on the moor, drinking with friends and family, and, yes, when running. I have to add, though, that it is not always the same qualities on display on each occasion.

Will I always be like this? Maybe. I can imagine being very old and there coming a day when the dog is shown the rabbit, as it were, and just goes, 'Nah, can't be bothered.' But right now, that is not in my character. Even when I tell myself it's okay to take it easy on a run, there is a bit of me that says, *Ian, your rightful place is further up the rankings. Fulfil yourself.* And that's the key, the desire for self-fulfilment. I don't think anyone can resist it. It's like we are water and we are compelled to fulfil ourselves by flowing downhill. We will one day reach the sea and lose all our identity but in the meantime, what is there to do but flow, and flow as fast as we can?

And to think I didn't want to run this morning! Sometimes we don't even recognise the path we are fated to follow.

11 | HUMILITY AND HUMILIATION

11 March

We are at Killerton. There is fog in the air and it is quite overcast but not cold. Ideal conditions – apart from the fact that the ground is sodden, making the course very muddy.

One man stands waiting on the start line, apart from the rest of us. He seems about forty-five, has classic good looks (with no grey), is about 6 foot 2 inches tall and wearing an Iron Man T-shirt. When I see him, he is looking over his shoulder with a wry smile, as if to say 'I'm the one to beat here today'.

Oliver and Alexander look at each other, then gather in a huddle with me.

'Dad,' says Alexander, 'your mission is to beat the man in the Iron Man T-shirt.'

'Or trip him up,' adds Oliver.

The whistle goes and we're off. Rising to the challenge of beating the man in the Iron Man T-shirt, I start fast. I charge through the middle of the puddles and the wettest mud. The local runners seem less familiar with the sloppy brown stuff and dance around it. I have to say it is the slipperiest I have yet seen at this course but at least it is wet enough that it doesn't suck your feet down like semi-dry mud does. And so I have a good run: I finish twenty-seventh out of 321 – well ahead of Mr Iron Man. Alexander wins the battle of the boys by about 30 seconds. But in age-graded terms, Oliver wins by a couple of percentage points, so he's quite happy.

As I was on the home stretch, a man in his sixties overtook me. Looking ahead, I could see a younger man in a red shirt, who had obviously finished the run, jogging back to support his family. The fellow in red shouted out, 'Go on, Dad!' Later I discovered that the older man shares the same surname – Minting – as the man who came first. Today the Minting family beat the Mortimers by a whole generation. It feels like a margin of victory equivalent to an innings defeat in cricket.

---

12 March

I head off to Clevedon to stay overnight with a friend, Jonathan Camp, who is planning to run the Bath half marathon with me. He is an art historian and an erstwhile philosophy teacher, and full of wisdom. He is also one of those mad people who swims in the sea every day of the year, including during the depths of winter. I don't join him for a dip but I do discuss race strategy with him. He has run the 'Bath Half' in 1 hour and 35 minutes before, so I pay attention. I tell him my target is 100 minutes. I also say I'm planning to do negative splits, meaning I will run the second half of the race faster than the first half. The plan is to set off steadily and see where we are after 7 miles. If I can get there within 52:30, I should have every chance of hitting my target.

We drive to the station and see a chap in running kit waiting to buy his ticket, so we start chatting. Just a pair of training shoes on a day like today is sufficient to spark a conversation. On the train, which is so crowded it is standing room only, we talk to a family who are going as supporters. The wife sees my book cover on my running shirt and takes a photograph for her Facebook page. Their nephew is running to raise money for charity because his mother has been diagnosed with cancer. There is a momentary pause in the conversation. I can't help feeling that their nephew is running magnanimously while I am doing so selfishly, even if the generosity of one act does not undermine the value of another.

When the crowd swarms off the train, we are swallowed up in an even bigger mass of people, many of whom are pinning their numbers on their shirts or tying their timing chips to their shoes. There is a real buzz of excitement in the air, movement everywhere. Jonathan is suffering somewhat from a metatarsal injury and so is not expecting to do a fast time, but he is as excited by the moment as I am. We take our place together in pen E, admiring the architecture of our surroundings as we wait for the start. After all, we are in Great Pulteney Street, one of the grandest Georgian streets in the whole of England. I look at the columns and architrave designed by Thomas Baldwin in the late eighteenth century and wonder why people generally believe in progress – that things are continually getting better. We've not seen any terraces as elegant as this built in England since the 1830s.

I do not look at the architecture after the start. I simply follow a mass of bobbing colourful shirts. There are so many people! It takes me over 2 minutes of shuffling forward to cross the line. Even after that, when we are jogging, we are moving far too slowly. There are crowds everywhere and a lot of good-natured jostling as runners sort themselves out. I wonder why I have to overtake so many of them – why have they been placed in this starting pen if they are so slow? I find myself nipping around the outside and weaving in and out of the colourful stream flowing down to the river. Despite this, my time for the first 2 miles is 14:38, and I feel heartened. I'm slightly ahead of schedule and it is not taking too much effort. The runners start thinning out as we run down towards Newbridge, and I speed up accordingly. My third mile is 7:06; my fourth 7:08. There's a short stretch of about a third of a mile after the bridge to the bend, after which we all turn back to the town centre. I see thousands of people ahead and think of that Alan Sillitoe book title, *The Loneliness of the Long-Distance Runner*. Frankly, running long distances these days is one way to make sure you will never be lonely again.

I pass the 10K mark in 45:05, with which I am happy. I reach the 7-mile marker at exactly 51 minutes – a minute and a half ahead of schedule. But then, suddenly, as I run towards Queen's Square for the second time, it all feels very hard. I cannot continue to run at this pace. I speed up on the next downhill slope but thereafter I struggle more and more. My eighth mile takes 8 minutes. And I have another 5 miles to go. How on earth am I going to continue? We are not even out of town yet; it is going to be difficult even to reach Newbridge. Oh, heavens above! I did not expect this. I feel so tired all I want to do is stop. What is happening to me?

I hear a siren. Marshals shout for us all to keep right as an ambulance goes past. Some poor runner has collapsed. He must have overreached himself. Is that going to be my fate if I carry on? Ventricular fibrillation, the failure of the electrical pulses in the heart, which causes the chambers to quiver rather than pump, leading to heart attack and normally death within a matter of minutes. I wish now I'd never read about it.

Nine miles done. One mile more I will be at Newbridge, where the road turns back to the town. All I need to do is to keep going. But this is hard, really hard. I run to the left-hand side of the road, not knowing whether I want to be sick or just spit. I do sums to keep my mind off how awful I feel. I did 7 miles in 51:00 – that leaves me 49:00 to do the last 6.1 miles if I am to finish in under a hundred minutes. At 8 minutes a mile, it is just possible. But the last mile was 8:09: those extra 9 seconds are not a good sign. And the half marathon has a sting in the tail: the last tenth of a mile, an extra 45 seconds of pain on top of the extreme discomfort you are already feeling after 13 miles. People are flocking past me now. *They* all knew how to pace themselves. *They* all heeded the advice to run negative splits. They might have been in my way at the start but they knew what they were doing.

At 9.5 miles I reach Newbridge with a grimace across my face. But we are not turning back to the town here. I have misremembered. There is another third of a mile until the turn. My mind is playing tricks on me. I want this to be over so much; I am really suffering. My watch buzzes to tell me the tenth mile is up: it has taken me 8:20. All hope of 100 minutes has well and truly gone. I can hardly envisage running another 3 miles at all, let alone at a faster speed. Even the shouts of those watching the race do not give me heart. But I refuse to give in. I tell myself that it is better to slow down than walk. This part of the town is grimy and industrial; its lack of inspirational qualities mirrors my lack of inspiration now in the same way that Great Pulteney Street reflected my optimism at the start. This is agony. I can't even tell you what is hurting. It is just that I am so tired. I think if it were a pain I'd be able to focus on it but this is just an overwhelming suffocation. I am not being stabbed but smothered. I keep checking my watch: 10.56 miles, 10.78 miles, 10.89 miles. Surely I should be at 11 miles by now? 10.97 miles. Will this mile never end?

Every single second is a struggle. The desire to stop pulses through my body. Other runners sweep past me, on both sides. Tall, short, male, female, bald, bearded, grey-haired, brunette, blond, red-headed, young and old. Shirts of all colours, with all sorts of messages. I begin to tell myself that I can still finish the race if I walk; it won't be the end of the world. In fact, no one will care apart from me. But therein lies a deep truth: I do care. I care so much it is enough to make up for everyone else here. I will not walk. No, I *shall* not walk. My watch tells me my pulse is hovering around 180 bpm. Someone once told me the fastest your heart can go safely is 220 minus your age: my maximum safe zone would thus be 171 bpm. But who told me that? Is it true? *Ventricular fibrillation...* I keep looking at my watch. Still not 12 miles. *Just hang on in there. Just make it to the end of this mile. Then there will be just one more to go.*

After another small eternity, the watch buzzes: 8:36 for the twelfth mile. Just 10 minutes more at this pace. But 10 minutes of *this*? You have got to be kidding! I would rather go for a dip in the ocean with Jonathan in January. How stupid I was to think I could keep running at sub-7:30 pace after doing just two long runs in the last 5 months. Parkruns have fooled me into thinking I am getting fitter when actually I am woefully underprepared for this distance.

I am almost delirious. I've lost the ability to add up my total time. I can't even remember what Great Pulteney Street looks like. So much for great architecture. There is a turn in the path ahead and I convince myself that the finish is just around the corner. Then I realise it is not the turning to the finish but just a roundabout. There are still a couple of hundred metres to go until the corner. I feel I am wobbling. When I do finally see Great Pulteney Street, the short distance to the finish line looks like a joke. I was expecting it to be just there, right in front of me. Instead the organisers have clearly thought it would be amusing to move it back a hundred metres, to make me run further. That's how stupid I am now: my thoughts are bumbling about and crashing into things, as if they were falling out of a tree, striking the branches of ludicrousness on the way down.

That thirteenth mile took me 8:53. But I don't care anymore. All I care about is that I can see the finish line. It is just a few metres away.

And it's over.

I stumble to the side of the road and lean against the temporary barriers. They shudder and scrape on the pavement as I sit down, in an uncontrolled way, with my back against them. My final time is 1:43:44. When I pick myself up and walk towards the runners' village, I accept a bottle of Lucozade gratefully. A lad offers me a finisher's medal. I can't talk: I gesture to him to put it around my neck. I walk to the fountain in Great Pulteney Street where I have arranged to meet Jonathan, and wait for him, hardly cognisant of the world around me. A man sees my shirt and says, 'Well done, Ian,' as he walks past.

'That was so tough,' I reply, finding my voice at last.

'Looks like it,' he says.

When Jonathan joins me, he is in a similar state. He too has failed to meet his target by a few minutes. We talk about the race on the way to the station and then on the train, having to stand because it is so full. Did we set out too fast? Clearly we did. Were we underprepared? Obviously we were. What should we say to our wives? He suggests that we tell them we both ran over the line with arms aloft having run it in 1:35:00. I laugh. But more seriously, what does our failure to meet our ambitions say? As we stand on the crowded train, he says, 'Here we are, each of us in his own way remarkable for the original things he *thinks*, and yet what do we do? Something that does not really require any thinking or originality. And we set ourselves physical targets which we then fail to achieve, making us like everyone else in the crowd.'

Thanks for the cheery thought, Jonathan.

At that moment, a young man nearby offers me a seat. 'You're more in need of this than me,' he says. I gratefully accept. It is the first time in my life I have been offered a seat on a train. If I did not feel so tired, it would be humiliating.

Humiliating.

That word sticks in my mind. There it meets its friend, the word 'humility', and they jog along together for a while, until we get off the train. As Jonathan and I walk back to the car, Humiliation and Humility accompany us. All this weekend, I have been given doses of humility. I felt it at being defeated by the margin of a whole generation by the Minting family yesterday. I experienced a moment of self-chastisement when the family on the train this morning remarked that their nephew was running the Bath Half for a cancer charity. Most of all, the race itself humbled me. It made me suffer. It forced me to take note of my misplaced self-confidence, and to acknowledge the lack of substance to my ambition. But it did not humiliate me. Nothing about this weekend was humiliating. Indeed, there is nothing here of which to be ashamed. At Killerton, I was in the fastest 10 per cent of the field. Hey, I *beat* the man in the Iron Man T-shirt! And in Bath, I came 2,206th out of 12,552 finishers – in the top 20 per cent, which isn't bad, especially when it was only my third long run of the year. I cannot think of a time in my life when humility and pride have gone so closely hand in hand.

If humiliation is making someone feel ashamed by injuring his pride, then learning humility in a way that simultaneously enhances his pride is a powerful thing. In fact, to make people recognise how much further they have to go to achieve their aims without undermining their self-worth – is that not at the heart of all good teaching?

12 | FUSSINESS

18 March

The weather is positively dreary – not dramatically terrible yet a long way from uplifting. The ground is sodden and it is still drizzling slightly. The sky is all of two dozen varieties of grey. The hues range from bleak and dull to weakly glowering and attempting (but not quite succeeding) to be ominous, depending on the direction in which you look. I know it's not going to be a quick run today. But then, it doesn't need to be. I'll be running with Oliver, and his companionship will more than make up for the struggle through the mud.

As I drink a coffee I read *The Times*' obituary of Ed Whitlock, who died on Monday at the age of eighty-six. He was the first person over the age of seventy to run a marathon in under 3 hours. When he was seventy-three, he ran the distance in 2:54:49. His last marathon time, at the age of eighty-five, was 3:56:33. He was disappointed. Everyone else was flabbergasted.

Oliver and I don't talk much as we drive into Exeter. When the whistle goes, I start jogging. I say to myself, *Just take this one easy. Resist the urge to compete.* I watch runners stream ahead of me. I let other people overtake. My time at the halfway mark is a full minute down on my best. Who cares? Today, I don't care. And if I don't care, then no one does. It is not important.

I look down at the slippery mud. This is like running through trifle. *Oh, but you're never happy, Ian. You don't like mud or wet grass. You don't like running up steep hills. You don't like steep downhills, very long straights, sharply twisting paths that slow you down, or repetitive laps. Come to think of it, you don't like uneven surfaces or ice, frost, sub-zero temperatures, harsh winds, gales, heavy rain, light rain, sleet, snow... If every course was set in beautiful grounds with a wide level tarmac path, you'd still find something to complain about. It would be too far from home or too crowded. The car park would be too expensive. And if it were absolutely perfect in every way, you'd go there too often and you'd start to hate it because it would become tediously familiar. Maybe you'd look forward to high winds and sleet then.*

My fussiness is like that of an irritating couple who spend half an hour discussing which is the best table in the restaurant, observing how dark this one in the corner is, or how poor the view is from that one. When I see people dithering like this, a little voice inside me shrieks, *For heaven's sake, it's only one meal; you're not going to spend the rest of your lives there.* I think the same about people selecting holiday accommodation: it *has* to have this facility, it must be near this place, the neighbours must not be too noisy, the pool not too crowded, et cetera. I can understand people looking at prisons this way – you might have to spend a long time in that little cell, and the character of your cellmate might be of very great concern to you – but restaurants and short-term accommodation, no. *So, come on, Ian, snap out of it. Just get on and run.*

Into the last quarter, back on the tarmac, and I seem to be catching a few people. That's a surprise. Maybe I'm actually running negative splits. Either way, I'm definitely catching them. And I pass a whole group. Now there are two more people ahead: can I catch them too? My competitive instincts take over. Then I realise my record of always finishing in the top 20 per cent of the field will be shot if I don't speed up. Little by little I draw closer to the two in front. One young man puts on a burst of speed. Someone else has saved all his energy for a last-moment dash to the line and runs past me. And then it is over. I am forty-third out of 217 runners, so I just managed to keep my top 20 per cent record by a whisker. And actually, I quite enjoyed it. Running at that comfortable pace was far more pleasurable than forcing myself to run fast.

I walk back to find Oliver. He is about half a mile from the finish and clearly not happy. When he has crossed the line and caught his breath, he explains.

'After two seconds, literally *two* seconds, I wanted to stop. I knew then it was not going to be a fast time.'

'Never mind, you did it. And you didn't stop. Some runs are like that: they are more about finishing than speed. My half marathon last weekend, for example.'

'Yeah, but that was a half marathon, that's different.'

'It's still a run. And your time today – well, you've done worse in the past.'

'Thanks for reminding me, Dad.'

'Hey, don't be downcast. Remember, no run is ever wasted.'

'That one was.'

'No, you're building muscle strength all the time. Do you think your muscles only grow when you set a personal best? Running slowly can be good for them too.'

'It was still a really bad time.'

'You can't say this was terrible just because it was not one of your best.'

'You do – all the time.'

'Well, you're probably still tired after your last cross-country run at school.'

'Thanks, Dad.'

Back home I crunch the numbers and see that, in comparative terms, that was my worst run of the year. It was Oliver's worst too. So, I might have enjoyed it more than usual but there was no satisfaction in it. There has got to be a balance between the two somewhere, surely? Actually, I suspect that satisfaction only comes from a performance that takes you out of your comfort zone. You can have satisfaction or enjoyment but not both at the same time.

I turn again to the obituary of Ed Whitlock. He used to train in his local cemetery because he would be too embarrassed to be seen running 9-minute miles in town.

As he put it, 'In the graveyard, the residents didn't care how fast I ran.' He certainly did not run for pleasure. 'I don't particularly enjoy this daily drudge. I'm not sufficiently organised or ambitious to do all the things you're supposed to do if you're serious.' And then I read a line that really grabs my attention. 'The more time you spend fiddle-diddling with this and that, the less time there is to run or waste time in other ways.' Ed ate and drank what he wanted, and didn't follow any specific training regimes; he didn't allow himself to be distracted by thinking that he'd run faster if he followed a specialist diet. I bet he'd have agreed with me in saying that the more time people spend choosing the best table in a restaurant, the less time they have for eating at it.

Fussiness might be part of the pursuit of perfection, of course. If you're Michelangelo and can afford to spend time painting every detail of the ceiling of the Sistine Chapel, it will definitely improve the end result. The Pope will be chuffed. But on the whole, being fussy or 'fiddle-diddling' just gets in the way. I know someone who has spent 30 years gathering source material for a biography of a medieval baron and found so much that she does not know where to begin. Sadly, she will never write that book. The more you curse the ground on which you're running, the more you are paying attention to things that will hold you back. You are talking yourself into running slowly. Likewise, the longer you feel you need to prepare, the longer you put off starting. Let others fuss about the details: your mission is to get the job done. And if you really don't like the surface under your feet, you know what you should do? Speed up. You'll spend less time running on it.

13 | NATURE VERSUS NURTURE

8 April

The clocks have changed, making the light last longer in the evenings, and the weather has eased into spring brightness, which is most welcome. About half a dozen positive reviews of my new book have been published. I feel quite upbeat. There's definitely a bounce in my step. But the next run is not about me; it's about Oliver. It will be his fiftieth parkrun.

I give him the choice as to where he wants to go. In the end he settles on Parke, the hardest course. That makes me smile because the first time he ran there, he exhausted himself on the 1-in-4 hill and declared he would never do it again. Alexander is also going to run with us. Even Sophie has agreed to put on her running kit to join our youngest in his moment of triumph. Elizabeth doesn't want to run but will come along to watch. At dinner the night before, I suggest the four of us run together. This does not go down well. Various objects are thrown at me across the table. Oliver looks at me solemnly and gives the verdict. 'Dad, I think that's a *very* bad idea.'

So, that's a no, then.

It is an utterly glorious day. Indeed, although the daffodils are fading now, and the snowdrops have long since gone, I don't think any spring has ever touched me quite like this one. The sheer exuberance of the green buds, the determination of fragile primrose flowers to shine as if they have just discovered the secret of everlasting youth, and the primeval recitative of the birdsong all sweep me away. If winter is drama and autumn history, then summer is fiction and spring pure poetry. I look at the garden and struggle to reconcile this beautiful fragment of nature with the horrors in the world and the dire predictions in the newspapers and the small-minded arguments on social media. I resolve not to mention politics, homework or GCSE revision – or book sales, book reviews, the Syrian War, Donald Trump, Brexit or landscape conservation. This will be a special day – just the family, the beauty of nature and Oliver's run.

A total of 142 of us line up at the start. When the whistle blows, I concentrate on maintaining a sustainable pace. When it comes to the 1-in-4 hill, I run up it in a positive fashion – no feeble pigeon-footing. My first mile is okay, considering it's still muddy. But then a couple of runners pass me. I am slowing slightly. One chap behind me is panting like a traction engine. I find the noise disturbing, and am very happy to let him go ahead. How differently human beings breathe! You'd have thought that, as it's pretty much the same chest action in all of us, we'd all sound the same.

But no. Some people breathe silently. Others somehow manage to wheeze, huff, puff and grunt all at the same time.

As soon as I finish I get a shout of congratulations from Elizabeth. I go to hug her. 'Er, no, Dad; you're all sweaty,' she replies. I give her a gentle hug anyway, and run back to find Alexander and Oliver, who are battling it out about half a mile from the finish. Alexander prevails. Oliver is five places behind him but sets a new course personal best. After they have got their breath back we all jog back to find Sophie, and run alongside her to the finish, giving her three cheers as she crosses the line.

The results come through on Elizabeth's iPhone while we are having breakfast at the café. I notice that the fast-running Minting family were also at Parke today. At Killerton 4 weeks ago, Mr Minting senior (who is in his late sixties) was one place ahead of me; today he finished one place behind. His son came first on both occasions. However, the older man won the age-grading battle, 72.3 per cent to his son's 70.0 per cent, which are impressive figures on this rough and steep course. The running genes are obviously pretty strong in the Minting family.

I look at my own children and think about this matter of genes. I wonder about the extent to which parents, who know their own inherent strengths, encourage those same qualities in their children. For example, a good runner, looking to see whether his son has inherited his ability, may well be particularly encouraging if the boy shows signs of being able to compete at a high level. I think of the dynasties of writers, like the du Maurier, Waugh and Amis families; I think too of father-and-son success stories in the motor-racing world, such as Graham and Damon Hill, and Keke and Nico Rosberg. Then there are the acting dynasties like the Redgraves, and the political ones, which are legion even in democracies that have no principle of hereditary power. I imagine that those who see their children blessed with the same gifts that they themselves possess are far more likely to make sacrifices to encourage their offspring. Bringing on children who have natural ability is therefore not just a matter of the right genes and the necessary hard work on the part of the youngster; it may well also involve an extraordinary level of encouragement from similarly talented parents.

It is this thought that prompts me to think about the whole nature-versus-nurture argument. We are encouraged by the media to think of this as an either/or matter, nature *or* nurture, largely because it seems on the face of it so absolute: either you are biologically programmed to do something well or you have been taught to do it. The cases chosen for television documentaries reinforce this polarisation. You know the type: two identical twin girls separated by adoption shortly after birth both go on to study the same subject at university, join the same profession and play volleyball until each of them marries a man with a beard called Rex and names their eldest son Fred. The case for nature over nurture, with the latter seemingly having no impact at all, is thus demonstrated. However, such stories obscure the fact that, for most of us, the division between nature and nurture is not that distinct. How do you separate a whole family's awareness of its genetic strengths and weaknesses into a question of nature or nurture? If I were a good runner and saw that one of my sons had inherited the running gene, of course I would encourage him to run. If I were no good at running and did not care for it, I would be less likely to do so, however talented he was. Thus it is not just a dose of nature *or* nurture, it is also the two mixed together. A maths teacher I know says the greatest difficulty she faces in teaching her less-talented pupils is that their parents say to them, 'Don't worry, love; I was never any good at maths either', thereby using a similar awareness of natural ability (or the lack of it) to nurture the child's continued failure to do well in the subject.

As we head back up the hill to the car park I look at my children walking on ahead. Sadly, none of us is gifted in the running department. But today's run has reminded me that I ought to look out for their natural talents whatever they may be, and to inspire them to make the most of them. For just as education by itself does not make success, natural talent can wither if it is not nurtured. It is the combination that matters, not a simplistic view that one is more significant than the other. Or, to put it another way, there is always room for encouragement.

14 | HEALTHY AMBITION

15 April

Yesterday a headline in *The Times* caught my eye. It said: 'One 60-minute run can add seven hours to your life'. Underneath it added: 'Running will do more to increase your lifespan than any other form of physical activity, according to an analysis of long-term studies on the exercise. Over the course of a lifetime it could add just over 3 years.' If you run and do other forms of exercise, you will lower your risk of premature death by 43 per cent. If running is your only physical activity, that figure is 30 per cent. If you don't run but only play other sports, it is just 12 per cent. Astonishingly, running is even better for you than giving up smoking.

There's nothing like news stories like this to encourage people to run – and, in the case of obsessive people like me, to overreach themselves.

Recently, the question of whether I was going to do a marathon cropped up in a conversation. The marathon is THE race we all want to have run, at least once. When the modern Olympic movement started in 1896, the 'long run' was seen as the great showpiece that bound together the athletes of the ancient world and those of today. That first modern marathon, which was won by a Greek water carrier, Spyridon Louis, was one of the most heroic and dramatic Olympic moments of all time. A stadium full of Greek patriots who had up to that point been denied a Greek gold medal were informed that an Australian was in the lead and likely to win – but then, to the amazement of all, Spyridon entered the stadium first, and the crowd went wild with excitement. The Olympic marathon still occupies centre stage in the minds of most amateur runners. Probably only the 100-metre sprint attracts more attention, but the brevity of that race means it is generally left to the specialists. There is no great merit in running 100 metres slowly. Completing a marathon, on the other hand, carries with it a badge of honour, no matter how fast you run.

As a result of this conversation, I decided to go for a 16.5-mile run, just to see what it might feel like. I set off very gently along the riverside path in Exeter, wary of the hot weather. However, I didn't take any water, which in retrospect was stupid. My very short running shorts started to chafe my inner thighs after about 3 miles. There wasn't much I could do about that, so I just carried on. After 7 miles, my times began to slip back by about 7 or 8 seconds per mile. My final mile took a full 10 minutes. I was exhausted. Blood was running down the inside of both legs, from my shorts to my socks. I probably looked like a middle-aged man successfully attempting to menstruate. My thighs were stinging terribly with all the salt from the sweat that had seeped into the gashes. The pain on my face was obvious to all the drinkers at cafés on the quay in the afternoon sun. Strollers and dog walkers stepped rapidly out of my way, staring at me as if I had just crawled out of the river covered in green scales. I was so glad to stop. Those 16.5 miles opened my eyes to just how hard it is to run long distances, and how gruelling a full marathon would be.

So I decided to do one.

Here's what I'm thinking. Over the next 6 months I am going to do at least one long run every week, building gradually. I'll begin by just trying to do a specific distance, not setting myself a time. I will run slowly, in order to enjoy it as much as possible. If I add a mile to the long run every fortnight, I should be able to run the full 26 miles by late September, when I will turn fifty. Fortunately my friends think I'm mad. Sophie doesn't approve either, which makes everything a lot easier. She thinks I'll give myself another stress fracture, or some other injury. If everyone was full of praise, it would just be down to me to live up to my resolution, which would be tough. But with their harrumphing, I will have the benefit of trying to prove them wrong. The idea of running a marathon is a challenge but to run one against people's expectations is an opportunity to surprise them – and everything becomes easier when you see it as an opportunity.

Alexander, Oliver and I arrive at Killerton and walk up the hill to the start of the parkrun. As we wait, I wonder how many ambitions of all different shapes and sizes are being brought to this place. So many whispers in the mind. Just as each runner will be nursing a niggling foot injury or a pulled muscle, or suffering from a bad night's sleep or a hangover, so too each one will have his or her aspirations. Many people will be ardent to run a personal best, or to break the 20-minute barrier, or the 30-minute one. I look around at all the faces: behind each smile and handshake lies an unspoken dream.

It makes me wonder whether actually that *Times* article about the three years' extra lifespan reflects more than just the physical benefits of running. For a start, did all those runners have the same lifestyle as non-runners? No, they were probably healthier than most people to begin with. Moreover, if you run with other people, or against the clock, it is likely that you are the sort of person who sets goals. If you do this for running, the chances are that you do so in other areas of life too. Perhaps it is really these ambitions that spur you on, and give you something to live for. Moreover, the basic virtue of hope is reflected in other ways too, not just how long we live. Many marriages fail, it seems to me, because husbands and wives cease to have a unifying ambition for their partnership. They lose sight of what they want to achieve together, and they accordingly lose the will to work together. The depression that follows may well be another demoralising factor that underpins the statistics in that *Times* article. Having things to look forward to – individually and collectively – is surely what keeps us alive.

No fewer than 456 runners are pursuing their dreams here today. When the whistle goes, a large number of them sprint ahead but I find myself unable to follow, hemmed in by many slower people. It takes me about 30 seconds to extricate myself from the bobbing crowd. After that I maintain a steady pace and finish in fifty-fourth place. Alexander does well, smashing his personal best. Oliver has not been so successful. In fact, it is the first time ever that Alexander's age grade has been higher than Oliver's. Oliver and I both congratulate him.

Can you teach people to have dreams? Or is ambition simply an aspect of personality? I would like to think that we can encourage people to want to improve. True, it is not easy to shape an individual's character; I've already written about how running reveals our irrepressibility. The challenges of reforming those whose violent tendencies lead them to prison are further testament to the fact. But the difficulty of suppressing someone's inclination to do something awful does not necessarily mean it is equally difficult to make somebody want to succeed in something worthwhile. Probably everyone running here today is encouraging everyone else to want to strive for more, for faster, for better.

Ambition is not always a good thing, I know. In certain circumstances it can lead to stress, financial ruin, controlling tendencies and, ultimately, a sense of failure and self-destruction. But, on the whole, most of us benefit from regularly focusing on what we want to get out of life. It gives us direction and a sense of purpose, enhances our psychological well-being and encourages those around us to support us in our endeavours, creating camaraderie. It is therefore hardly surprising that runners tend to live longer than non-runners. But, of course, one of the most beautiful things about the ambition to run faster is that you don't actually need to achieve it. You might say even that the most perfect dream – the one that will keep you alive the longest – is the one which remains tantalisingly just out of reach.

15 | TOO GOOD TO BE TRUE?

22 April

Oliver is playing chess this week, so today's parkrun team is just Alexander and me. We arrive in Exeter early and hang around smiling with everyone else as the crowd gathers. When the briefing begins, we applaud a woman doing her 100th run. We welcome someone who has come all the way from Durham. We greet like-minded strangers with open arms. It is all very positive, so much so that I feel there is something a bit too 'goody two-shoes' about all this running together. It is an impression that is heightened by the community message that is emailed out to all parkrunners every week, with stories of how someone overcame obesity through parkrun or started running when recovering from a brain haemorrhage. Around me I see printed running vests that have a charity logo or proclaim a cause, such as fighting cancer or Alzheimer's. I feel very slightly out of place – a louche, hard-drinking fox standing in the midst of three hundred wholesome chickens.

The keen athletes on the starting line are about as far from rock 'n' roll as you can get. Lightweight, easy-breathing running vests instead of leather jackets. Gel-cushioned running shoes rather than cowboy boots. Garmin watches and Fitbits in place of electric guitars. I don't suppose a great many young people here drink that much; this isn't exactly a 'Beer Mile' event (more on those below). As for drugs, these folk don't look as if they'd know how to roll a cigarette, let alone a joint. The nearest thing I can see to a symbol of the counterculture is a huge tattoo across a young woman's shoulders, revealed by the singlet she is wearing. Oh, and there's a 'Vegan Runners' shirt. That really says it all. The gritty hardcore aren't just interested in their fitness, they're into saving the planet too. '

Has there ever been a 'bad boy' of running? Runners don't seem to fall into that category. Famously, tennis has had its rebels – Ilie Nastase, Jimmy Connors and John McEnroe in the seventies and eighties; and more recently Nick Kyrgios. Motor racing has attracted a number of womanising, hedonistic heroes – James Hunt particularly comes to mind – and golf has John Daly, whose alleged misdemeanours put him in a similar category in the public imagination. So many talented footballers and rugby players could be listed as reprobates that it is not necessary to single out an individual. Yet running? I can't think of anyone who qualifies. Asking around, my friend and fellow runner Bob Small suggests David Bedford. In his heyday in the 1970s, Bedford drank a couple of pints of beer regularly 'and five or six on Friday and Saturday nights depending on the race schedule'.[2] Other reported incidents include him spending the night behind bars with six teammates when he was captaining England at the World Cross Country Championships, and ringing up the organiser of the first London Marathon (1981) hoping to take part after being persuaded to run the night before the event when drunk in a nightclub. But, in marked contrast to his notoriety, for many years he organised the London Marathon, and gave tirelessly to the sport. If he deserves the title 'bad boy of running', it is only because he has no clear rivals.

So, what about people competing in the Beer Mile? As you probably know, this involves competitors drinking a standard American 355 ml can of beer (while stationary), then running one lap of a 400-metre track, stopping, opening another can and drinking it, then doing the whole routine of stopping, opening, drinking and running twice more. That's 2½ pints of beer in 1 mile. It sounds a laugh – and it's exactly the sort of thing I'd have done at the age of nineteen – but some people take it very seriously. According to the Beer Mile official website (www.beermile. com), the world record is 4:34, set by the Canadian Corey Bellemore.[3] Wow! The English record is 4:47 set by Dale Clutterbuck. Mr Clutterbuck has also done a Beer Mile in which he drank a whole pint before each quarter mile – 4 pints in all – and then ran the distance in 4:57. This isn't some sort of lads' night out, racing between pubs: it's athletes performing in singlets and shorts on race tracks at near-Olympic speeds, with specific rules as to the strength of the beer (at least 5 per cent alcohol). Bellemore on the booze is only 12 seconds per lap slower than Hicham El Guerrouj's non-alcoholic world record. If beer milers vomit at the end – as they often do – they apologise profusely, displaying impeccable manners for people who are both inebriated and exhausted. The plain fact is that athletes are pretty much all good guys and girls. If you try searching on the internet for immoral track athletes, the results will all be drugs cheats – not party animals or hotel-room-wrecking rebels.

The whistle goes. I know that Alexander will stick behind me as long as he can, so I do not start too fast. I want to encourage him. As we enter the woods, I concentrate on the long line of runners ahead, trying to cut the lead with every step. I recognise a man about 50 metres in front of me who can run 5K in under 20 minutes, so I do my best to catch up with him. But then we enter the field and I see where the cones have been placed. To do the full distance here you need to run all the way around the extreme perimeter. These cones have been placed well inside that line. I know from experience that this results in a shortening of the circuit by about 30 metres. I have a quandary: which is the more important – my position or the distance? In my heart, there is no option. I must do the full distance. Otherwise my time won't mean anything.

I run to the very edge of the field. Glancing to my right I see that no one else is following; they are all keeping to the shorter, marked route. By the time I rejoin the line of runners on the straight, seven or eight people have overtaken me and the 20-minute man is about 80 metres ahead. Further on there is another swerve in the course that has been smoothed out by the person who laid out today's cones; I follow the original line and watch another runner pass me. Now I am more than a hundred metres behind my 20-minute marker.

It is not that anyone here is cheating. Many won't know the course, and those who have GPS watches will need to have run this route before to learn that cutting off the corners like this will leave them short of the full 5K. Realistically, if you want to compete, you have no choice but to run the course as laid out. But the truth is that I am being even more conscientious than the goody-goodies. I think I will have to have a stiff drink when I get home to remind myself who I really am.

I finish thirty-first in a time of 20:37. My age grade is 71 per cent – my best so far this year. But even better is to see Alexander finishing just 3 minutes behind me. He is very pleased with himself, and I am ecstatic for him. Everyone is joyful for everyone else, it seems. Even today, when a purist could accuse most of the runners of not completing the full 5K, such a criticism is the last thing on anyone's mind. We all want each other to do well and be happy.

The feeling as we head off to have our barcodes scanned is a sort of total immersion in goodwill. Far from thinking of myself as a fox amongst chickens, I have been totally converted to the chickens' view. My critical faculties have grown feathers. On what basis was I so cynical? Some things cannot simply be written off as 'too good to be true'. There is a genuine uplifting feeling following such a run, which you can ignore but you cannot deny.

Although running is not normally thought of as a team sport, it certainly brings people together in a collective desire to do well. We become a team. My sons and I are each driven by a strong individualism yet we all understand the camaraderie of taking part in a race. When at the end of the afternoon a very tired Oliver comes home from his chess tournament, I see he is carrying a trophy. Undefeated in all his games, he came first. The smile on his face says it all. Once again we share the kindness of congratulations. He too has looked up our results and compliments his older brother. 'That's going to be a hard time to beat,' he says, acknowledging Alexander's achievement with sincerity and admiration.

Running shows us a world in which hard work and natural talent pay dividends, and in which conflict, dishonesty and cynicism have no place. It allows us to contrast a society in which everyone is trying to encourage everyone else with one in which people are quick to criticise their fellow competitors – and you don't need to be a genius to see that an uplifting society is far better than a downplaying one. Yes, a few professionals take banned substances and run times that are indeed 'too good to be true', but forget them. Their running is the false sort, full of greed and guilt. In contrast, true running allows you to step into a world of virtue. And that is something you can't get from any drug.

16 | MARRIAGE

29 April

Last Wednesday was our twentieth wedding anniversary. As mentioned before, one of my New Year's resolutions was to celebrate the occasion 'in style'. So I told Sophie to pack for one night away and took her up to London to revisit the church where we were married, and to the pub in Covent Garden where we first met. Best of all, however, I had booked the same table in the dining room at the Ritz where we got engaged. After all these special returns, and a party for our friends in Moreton, I reckoned I could consider that I'd succeeded in fulfilling my resolution. The only thing that remained to be done was to run a parkrun together.

'No way,' was her reply.

Apparently, there's nothing romantic about struggling for 3 miles amidst a horde of other sweating, puffing people. Especially when she wants to have a lie-in.

As a result, it's just the indomitable duo of Oliver and me heading down the road to Parke this morning. Before we head off, however, I go for a preliminary run. A few days ago, I went for a 17.5-mile jog. It was both rewarding and encouraging. However, a day later, I realised I had injured myself. My left femur felt as if someone had attacked it with an iron bar – except the pain was *inside* the leg. When I tried to run on it, it hurt so much I had to stop. I haven't run since. Therefore I am somewhat apprehensive as I launch myself into a half-mile fast downhill, thinking that if my leg is going to stop me anywhere it will be here. It hurts with every impact – but not quite enough to prevent me from trying to run.

Sophie would call it an unwise decision. Although I run quite fast – finishing only 16 seconds outside my all-time best time at Parke – I am in considerable discomfort the whole way. It seems that people who run develop very high pain thresholds for any ailment that might be connected with their running. The level of agony that would drive most normal people to phone for an ambulance simply makes us worry about how we are going to overcome the problem and still put in a good time. Our minds are set on the higher goal. But, as I drive home, this very fact seems to reflect the reality of a good marriage. Just as we don't immediately think of stopping when injured but try to find a way through the pain, we don't immediately think of walking out on our partner when we hit a rocky patch but search for solutions. In fact, more and more aspects of today's run seem to relate to marriage. Right at the start, I was surrounded by other people and held back by the crowd. That rings true to the days when in our teens and twenties we have so many relationships in quick succession that we have no way of sorting out what we're looking for in our eventual life partner. When it came to the 1-in-4 hill today, I charged straight up it, despite the pain. You can compare that too to the way we behave in the early days of a relationship: showing off, full of energy and enthusiasm. But eventually that energy diminishes and you start to slow up. Then it is important to keep disciplined, to run with all the style and strength that you can. Swing your arms, don't allow your stride to shorten. Set targets and try to close in on them gradually. Above all else, keep going. The most successful marriages are not made by those who sprint off in a blaze of glory and then, having reached a point of exhaustion, start to walk. They are made by those who keep going steadily and never slip from promise to disappointment.

I wonder if runners enjoy longer marriages? They have the benefit of knowing that sometimes a partnership is not all easy-going and that it requires patience and endurance. They understand that you will have bad patches and that you can work your way through them. They know that the important thing is always to keep going. Perseverance is what you need in both running and marriage.

I park the car and, walking up the garden path, plan how to arrange my ideas into an account of today's run. I enter the house and put my keys down on the work surface in the kitchen. Sophie's there, with a big smile on her face. 'Guess what?' she says. 'I slept in until ten past nine. Nine hours' sleep. I can't remember the last time that happened.'

I smile. That's the essence of a good marriage: that she could still be asleep when the whistle went this morning.

It might not be romantic in a traditional sense but when you think about it, it is probably more conducive to marital bliss than dinner at the Ritz. The secret is not to shackle yourselves together with heavy romantic chains, which will only hold you back. Rather, it is to bind yourselves gently together with the longest, finest gossamer thread, which will stretch to endless lengths to accommodate both of you. And never break.

17 | RUNNING IS YOUR FRIEND

6 May

This is not good. Every time I put my foot on the ground, my femur hurts like a bruise being struck with a hammer. Is it another stress fracture? Oh, heavens, I hope not.

But I suspect it is.

As a precaution I did not run or walk any distance all week. No weight-bearing exercise at all. I've felt myself getting weaker and weaker, every day, and heavier too.

This is why I have been longing for today's parkrun, at Torbay Velopark. I feel as if Oliver and I are going to visit a much-loved old friend of the family, who will cheer us up. I don't feel any nervousness, I don't care how fast or slow I run; I just want to get out there and go for it. And to see Oliver run too. His hope of breaking the 25-minute barrier is one of the rocks on which I am steadying myself at the moment. This week he could do it, I tell him, as we drive to Torbay.

The idea that running is a 'friend' is something that has not occurred to me before. This is perhaps not surprising.

It does not always act in a very friendly way. It has frequently made me feel like hell. It's never told me jokes or bought me a drink. Right now, it is the reason why every step I take is painful. But when I am deprived of its company, if only for a week, I miss it. It comes around regularly and checks on how I am. It looks after me, gives me pride and makes me leaner, stronger, fitter, healthier, and – according to some recently published research that was reported in *The Times* last week – keeps my brain more active. It is a companion when lonely and a joy when I'm low in spirits. If music be the food of love, then running is the wine of pride.

Off we go, and after a few hundred metres the pain subsides, so I can put it out of my mind. At about the 1.5-mile mark, I glance back, looking for Oliver. He is doing well, no more than a minute behind me. It gives me a thrill to see him there. Alexander had his moment of glory 2 weeks ago; today it is Oliver's turn. But how well can he do? Can he break 25 minutes? At the next turn I shout encouragement to him – only to hear him cheering me on at exactly the same moment. 'Go on, Dad!'

When the next person comes up to overtake me I sense his speed and stay with him. He is in his thirties, in a blue and white shirt. Together we run abreast of each other for about half a mile before his greater strength carries him past me. I continue to push hard, however, feeling the pain in my leg but not wanting to let Oliver down. Another runner overtakes, and another. As I enter the last straight, a teenager goes ahead of me and although I try, I cannot catch him. I finish fourteenth, which is okay, considering my leg.

But where is Oliver?

I limp back and see him still loping along. I shout at him to speed up: if he keeps going he's going to break 25 minutes. I haven't been timing him but he must be about 2 minutes behind the 23-minute pacer. I shout at him even more urgently. He puts in that little bit more effort, and finishes fifty-fourth.

'That was *definitely* under twenty-five minutes,' he declares when he has got his breath back. 'The twenty-five-minute pacer was ages behind me.'

I had forgotten about the second pacer. There was an enormous gap between the two. Either the 25-minute pacer was running too slowly or the 23-minute pacer was much too fast. Not wanting him to be disappointed, I say, 'Let's hope they put the results up soon.'

When the finalised times are posted online, I scroll down to fifty-fourth place and see Oliver's name. He ran 23:57.

I am so pleased for him. I hug him and feel like dancing around the room. After so many weeks of trying, such a result is so sweet.

'You didn't just break twenty-five minutes, you broke twenty-four.'

My joy at both of my sons breaking 24 minutes in the space of a fortnight – and especially at Oliver doing it after such a long time doggedly trying – carries me through the whole day. It is not that he ran a particularly fast time but rather that he set himself a goal, kept at it all the way through the winter, and finally achieved it. And no one will ever be able to take that away from him.

Running is indeed an old friend. If all the world should turn against us, we will still have running. It doesn't prefer me over you, or you over me, or anyone over anyone else, even if he or she is faster. And although I must now say goodbye to my friend for another week, in order to let my femur heal as best it can, we will meet again next Saturday. I look forward to the occasion. For running serves that essential function that all good friends should provide when things are difficult.

It doesn't allow us to forget our true priorities.

18 | RUNNING FOR OFFICE

13 May

It is the weekend of the Mortimer History Society conference in Ludlow, Shropshire. This organisation is devoted to discovering and sharing the history of the medieval Mortimer family who dominated the Welsh border from the time they arrived here with drawn swords and grim determination in the 1070s until the main line of the family died out in 1425. I know what you're thinking. No, I am not called 'Mortimer' because of them: my father's family comes from Devon. However, these Mortimers of the Welsh Marches are all our ancestors because one of them, Roger Mortimer, 1st Earl of March, who was hanged for treason in 1330, had twelve children, including eight daughters. One of those daughters had about fifteen children and another had nine. By 1500 Roger had so many descendants that he is an ancestor of everyone of English descent living in England today, as well as a good proportion of those living overseas. Coincidentally, you can say the same thing about Edward II, the king whom Lord Mortimer deposed in 1327. I quite like that irony.

A political argument almost 700 years ago has dissolved into the lifeblood of the nation. No wonder we are all so sceptical of our political leaders. Anyway, I am in Ludlow as the vice-president of the society. That means I must somehow combine the conference with a run. And then on the way home, I will take part in the Hereford half marathon.

It turns out that the local parkrun is in Mortimer Forest, the old hunting ground of the medieval Mortimers. They rode around it on horseback, chasing deer and game. I am going to run around it on foot, chasing a time of 23 minutes.

The augurs are not good, however. Not only does my femur still hurt, and is much worse after last week's run, the pub opposite the hotel in which I am staying has live music until late. My room is far too hot and the music much too loud. When the pub closes, several drunk people start shouting at each other in the street. Then they start smashing things. I hear loud thuds, car alarms and glass breaking. Eventually some local security men persuade the miscreants to go on their way, but it takes ages before I nod off. And then I wake up at 3.53 a.m. I lie there, unhappily not asleep. Streetlight clings to the edges of the curtains until daylight comes. At 7 a.m. I get up and drive to the forest.

There is something magical about this part of England in the early morning. It has been raining and the smell of the soil and the woods is enticing, enriching and poetic. The bluebells are out. Raindrops are glistening where they cling to leaves. All through this part of the forest there are pine trees offering up a sweet smell. I walk around in the sun, noticing such natural intricacies as a wet spider's web sparkling in the darkened hollow of an upturned tree root, and the chorus of birdsong greeting the morning enthusiastically – as if it is the first time these birds have ever seen the sun rise. It feels primeval, modern and eternal, all at the same time.

People start arriving, jogging silently in their bright colours beneath the trees. They seem a little reluctant to say hello, eyeing me with a kind of caution. I wonder if it is because I am wearing the running shirt with my book covers on it. Or maybe it's because I look exhausted. I greet them anyway. No reason why a little bit of Devon friendliness should not follow me wherever I go.

We gather for the start. The men here look very competitive. Straight away one athletic-looking chap races ahead, seemingly determined to break the course record. Five other runners head off after him. I follow them, feeling a thudding pain with every step. I think about trying to keep up for about 30 seconds – and then ask myself *what am I doing, hurting myself like this?* So I settle into a more manageable pace, feeling strangely happy even though I'm in pain, waiting for people to overtake me. Gradually they do; I don't care. I just pretend I'm the only one here, running beneath the trees, in my eponymous forest.

It is a punishing course, one of the hilliest in the country. There are inclines and descents that take it out of you, repeatedly. On the second lap, a man about my age comes up alongside and we keep each other company going up the last hill until he draws ahead at the top. As we descend the last slope, a deer that has been lurking in the shadows of the trees attempts to dash across our path. Suddenly it sees us, and turns on its ankles, leaping back into the forest. *There goes a descendant of the medieval hunters' quarry*, I say to myself, happy to see it go free. I watch it run through the woods, bounding with a fluency that makes us human runners look as awkward as cows running across a field when a train speeds past.

I finish 16th out of 87, almost 6 minutes slower than the first-placed runner. They are tough up here in Ludlow, I tell you. I can imagine a medieval ancestor looking at me and curling his lip in disdain – before stabbing his roasted meat with his eating knife and devouring it, glaring at me, with blood and juices dripping from his beard.

But the beauty of today is not what happened here, it's what my sons did back home in Devon. In my absence, Alexander and Oliver set their alarms, caught the bus into Exeter, and did the parkrun there. How many teenage boys would do that first thing on a Saturday morning? For a moment I have a glimpse of them running together after I am gone. When I'm no more than a memory, they'll be side by side. And I hope their children will run too, and their children, until that memory of me fades, and, like a sputtering candle, goes out. And the world I have known is finally at peace.

---

14 May

Guess what? The pub opposite has another live band performing. The music stops at midnight but the raucous, drunken swearing continues for another hour. And then it turns to more aggressive shouting. I roll over, knowing I am going to be exhausted before I begin the half marathon tomorrow. Gradually the audience dissipates around 1 a.m. But at 3.30 I awake to hear two people shouting at each other in the empty, echoing street. I drift off again and wake at 4.40, and then lie awake for the next 2 hours. When I get up I feel like I'm tiptoeing along a cliff edge of tiredness, liable to fall off at any minute.

I check out of the hotel and drive to Hereford Leisure Centre. One lady shows me a map of the course. 'It's the last time you'll be able to run along this lane,' she tells me. 'They're going to build twelve hundred houses there later this year.' Shortly afterwards I strike up a conversation with an affable fellow called Stuart, who has just had a baby daughter. He and his wife are collecting a box of keepsakes from the year of her birth to give to her when she is older. His finisher's medal from today will go into that box.

About five hundred of us set off in the sunshine. With my leg in pain, and being so out of condition, I know this will be a slow race. But my prime concern is to avoid making the mistake I made in Bath, in running too hard too early. Today is just about finishing another of the five half marathons I've resolved to do this year. I carefully set off at about 8 minutes per mile, happy to be moving along the tree-lined lanes. I grit my teeth against the ache in my femur for the first mile or so, but then, little by little, it bothers me less. After 2 miles there is a long hill, which requires effort. Going down the far side is lovely, and I am quite happy. But then it starts to get tougher again. *Never mind, I've saved energy, I'll be fine.* I reach the 7-mile mark in a steady time of 53:40.

At that point, just like in Bath, everything suddenly starts to feel much, much tougher. I count down the next 3 miles and see each one getting slower. Then with relief I see the 10-mile mark. There's only the equivalent of a parkrun to go. This next mile is a straight main road. Ahead I see other people flagging too. My eleventh mile is 8:33. The twelfth has a slight hill, which forces me to go even slower. The last mile also sees me struggling at first but, when I see the crowd around the finishing ground, I start to sprint – and it feels good. In fact, it feels great! In the last 400 metres I overtake five other runners. Then I cross the line and have to lie down. I forget to stop my stopwatch. Lack of sleep and a shortage of long-distance training have left me exhausted.

I wait until Stuart finishes, congratulate him and say goodbye. Then I make my way back to the car. The journey home will take at least 3½ hours. I can barely stand up. The sun is out, the birds are singing, it's a lovely Sunday afternoon – but I am too tired to drive. I've only had about 6 hours sleep in the last 54.

But I have no choice.

As I drive I try to keep myself awake by scratching myself, singing loudly, hitting my leg and thinking about the run.

It was very satisfying in some ways. Although it was the slowest competitive half marathon I've done – I later learn that my time was 1:47:23 – I completed it. What's more I did so in a controlled and measured way, not pushing myself to the point of self-torture. I was able to take my desperate tiredness into account, as well as my injury and the hills on the course, and I never once thought I'd have to stop. It was a true lesson in self-discipline because, with every step of the race, I was both reasoning that I *could* control my physical state and, at the same time, seeing myself benefit from doing so.

As I drive and sing and slap myself, I think of Stuart's baby daughter, and what she will think of the blue-ribboned finisher's medal she'll find in her box of keepsakes in about 18 years' time. Probably not a lot. She'll know that her dad used to run half marathons – he's bound to mention it at some point. Maybe she'll have run a few races herself by the time she puts that box away on the top of her wardrobe, for it to gather dust. By then no doubt Stuart and his wife will be thinking of grandchildren. I contrast their thinking forward with my harking back yesterday to our ancestors. Why do we – and many tribes around the world – think of ancestor worship? Why do we never think of worshipping our descendants? After all, they are our future: if anyone will remember us and what we do, it will be them. Of course, there's no guarantee that we'll have any descendants. Maybe we will wipe ourselves out in a nuclear war. Perhaps our children will be the last of our line. While we can picture our forebears as ghosts looking down on us from heaven or some other ethereal place, we cannot picture those yet to be born. Who knows what faces, ambitions and instincts they might have? They have no identity; their parents have yet to meet. You can't believe in something or someone that you know does not exist.

I am nodding at the wheel. I stop at every service station on the motorway, and walk around, if only for a minute, just to keep my mind alert. The same self-preservation strategy that I employed on the run is called for – except that now everything is much more serious.

Sing, sing. Slap, slap. *Breathe deeply. Concentrate.*

The lack of clarity about our descendants is perhaps one of the reasons we think very little of the future. When politicians campaign for an election, they appeal to the voters of today, not those of 100 years' time. Yet if we wish to protect this planet so that those dwelling here in the future will have a good standard of living, we ought to be considering them and their needs too. To compare the human race to an actual running race, we are charging ahead with no regard for how far we have yet to go. We are not pacing ourselves at all, and certainly not eking out our resources. If we really could see eternity stretching away ahead of us, we would not be so welcoming of a world increasingly filled with gadgets, fashions and fads – and hungry housing estates where there were once quietly productive fields. We would see all these things as unsustainable, like running too fast at the start of a race.

That brings me to the election coming up on 8 June. If people really want to safeguard the world for their descendants, then they need to build a society that knows how to pace itself. At present, all the campaigning is about what will happen over the next five years. Just *five* years. Even 'long-term' local plans are only meant to cover the next 20 years. If we want to be in a fit state in another hundred years or so, when our grandchildren's sons and daughters will be the ages we are now, we need to plan for society then too. We need to set targets that are not about the immediate future but more distant objectives, and understand that we have no option but to deny ourselves certain things in the short term in order to achieve them.

Of course, it is no good if only politicians understand this. The voters need to get the message too – otherwise they'll just vote for whoever is offering them jam today. So it would be good if everyone would run, in the hope they might develop the long-term vision the world needs. But I wish I could take the members of both Houses of Parliament with me on my next half marathon. Let's face it, if they are not able to conserve their own resources for just 2 hours, what hope is there that they will conserve those of the nation over the next 100 years?

19 | VOLUNTEERING

20 May–3 June

According to my physiotherapist, I am suffering from a 'femoral diaphysis stress fracture'. I failed the 'hopping test' (the measure of pain when hopping on the affected leg) and the 'fulcrum test' (the measure of pain when a weight is put on the femur pivoted on a ridge). So I won't be doing any running for the next few weeks. Last time I had a stress fracture, I carried on running on it for 4 months and the recovery did not start until I stopped altogether. It then healed relatively quickly. So, the plan is that I shall do no running or long-distance walking for 4 weeks, and then I will do a second round of tests.

I can still fulfil my target of taking part in 45 parkruns, however, by volunteering as a marshal. I enjoy the role. You get a totally different view of the event when you see the whole crowd go past. Indeed, you feel like you share the day with everyone, not just the small number of people who run with you. Also, you see where you would appear in the long stream of runners. In my case, although I often finish 4 minutes behind the leader, a marshal at the halfway point would see me appear just 2 minutes after him – and long before the majority of the chasing pack.

On one occasion, I arrive at Parke early and chat to the run director. I ask her how many people are available to help each week and she tells me that she is always struggling to make up the numbers. 'If everyone who runs here regularly were to volunteer just three times per year,' she says, 'then there would be no problem.' I tell her how grateful we are that she and several other people volunteer every single week. After all, on average, people need to help out once for every ten runs they do for the system to operate. Without that ratio, everything grinds to a halt.

As I watch the runners go through, spattering me with mud, I wonder how many of them have volunteered in the past. When I am able to check later, I see the variation is quite remarkable. I look at the first ten finishers. One has helped out nine times, another six, another five, another four, and a fifth, three times. Or, to be fair to those who haven't run that often, of the seven people in the ten who have run 20 times or more, five have volunteered at least once. That's a pretty good proportion, five out of seven. The only downside is that the two exceptions have run in excess of 60 times each and have never once volunteered.

I look further down the list to see how many other experienced parkrunners have given up their time. The next name with more than 20 runs to his credit has done 110 parkruns. He normally runs in the south-east. And how many times has he volunteered? Sixty-six! Wow! That's impressive. That's six times the proportion needed to keep things ticking over. The person who finished next after him has also run 110 parkruns: he has helped out 28 times. Bravo. Sadly, the next runner has not helped once in more than 50 runs.

I look at all the roles performed by the man who has volunteered 66 times. These include run director, pre-event setup organiser, marshal, token sorter, barcode scanner, timekeeper, backup timer, distributer of finish tokens, pacer and post-event closedown organiser. Such a list makes me think of all the tasks that worker bees perform. They collect pollen and carry it back to the hive; build new cells and repair old ones with wax; seal the honey in; clean cells for re-use; build brood cells for the next generation; nurse the larvae; feed the drones; attend the queen; remove dead bees and larvae from the hive; fan the hive to keep it cool; and guard it against predators. Yet there is no chance of their own progeny enjoying the benefits of their labour. Worker bees are sexless females who slave away for the benefit of the whole of their community. There's nothing in it for them individually; they will not have children. If anyone ever asks you, 'Does altruism exist?' and tries to tell you that all actions are basically selfish, just tell them about worker bees.

The disparity reminds me of something Oliver witnessed after a recent parkrun. 'One of the organisers suggested to a runner that she might like to volunteer to be a marshal some time, and the runner replied that, no, she wouldn't, because she doesn't get anything out of volunteering.' Oliver told me this in a sort of state of shock, and I understood why. You just don't expect people at a parkrun to be so selfish.

'That's ridiculous!' I replied. 'You can't hold the event if you don't have volunteers. How did they leave things?'

'The organiser didn't say anything,' he said. 'She just walked away.'

Before I started running parkruns, I generally nodded in agreement when someone declared that everyone in modern society has a selfish streak, and that even the most generous philanthropist gets something out of giving. My subsequent experiences have made me reconsider this. For a start, it is unnecessarily cynical to put the accent on the selfishness of an act and to belittle the generosity. Who on earth has the right to do that? More importantly, highlighting the selfish streak reduces everyone to the same level of self-interest. This is wrong, for there is a whole spectrum of altruism. It ranges from those who indulge themselves at other people's expense and offer nothing in return, to those who ask for very little and give enormous amounts back. Indeed, some people are so generous that, like worker bees, they give everything and only ask for the satisfaction of helping others. Even if it is true that we all act out of self-interest to some degree or other, we should not forget that this world is full of generous people as well as parasites, and that there is an important moral difference between the two.

But what do you say to the person who refuses to help his or her community? What *should* you say to people who have the nerve to declare they won't help because 'there's nothing in it' for them? What *can* you say to such people?

That organiser was right. You can't say anything. You can only walk away.

20 | SOME RUN TO REMEMBER, SOME TO FORGET

16 June

More than five weeks have now passed since I last ran. I intended to go for a jog last weekend but a journalist who came to Devon to interview me said something that made me think twice. She used to be a runner herself. On one occasion, after incurring an injury, she went to see a physiotherapist. Although he recommended that she should refrain from running for 12 weeks, she resumed much sooner than that, and made her injury worse. 'Ah, you amateurs, you're impossible!' he exclaimed when he next saw her. 'If I tell professionals not to run for twelve weeks, they do what I say. Amateurs always think they can start early.' So I restrained myself for another week.

But then something happened.

As you are no doubt aware, Grenfell Tower was a 24-storey concrete block in west London. Two nights ago, a man's fridge-freezer caught alight on the fourth floor. This set light to his kitchen. He alerted his immediate neighbours and the fire brigade was called just before 1 a.m. They put out the fire – or thought that they had done so – but unknown to them, the cladding and insulation applied to the external walls was smouldering. Everyone remained in their flats, as instructed by fire notices in the building. The firefighters themselves and the 999 call centre operators reinforced this advice to stay put. Suddenly the cladding and insulation caught alight. Fire spread rapidly up the outside of the structure. By 1.30 a.m. flames had reached the very top storey. Yet still people remained where they were, even as the fire swept around their homes, breaking windows and igniting the contents. Smoke from the burning flats below swirled up the central stairwell and poured under doors. Witnesses on the ground watched families using flashlights, desperately trying to draw attention to their plight. They heard people screaming, especially children whose high voices carried over the cracking and roaring of the fire. Then, gradually, the screams subsided and the flashlights disappeared until there was only the noise and glare of the fire mercilessly consuming the vestiges of so many homes, hopes, loves and lives.

So far this book has largely consisted of lessons in life that have been revealed or inspired by some aspect of a run. Now the flow of meaning has changed direction. The insights do not flow *from* running but back into it. Just as the lessons that I learned from running forced me to start writing, so the messages of this tragedy require me to start running.

But why? Why has the Grenfell Tower tragedy had this effect on me? Why not the Portuguese forest fires that killed more than 60 people in their cars just 3 days later? What connects Grenfell Tower specifically with my wanting to run?

I think it is a combination of several things. First, it is at least partly due to the archetypal horror of being trapped in a burning tower block with no way out. That is my absolute nightmare. It is partly due also to the injustice of the council using flammable panels to clad and insulate the building rather than slightly more expensive non-combustible ones. To that I'd add the lack of provision for fire safety, the lack of sprinklers and an ineffective fire alarm. These things show a scant regard for lives. But perhaps the main reason is that many people died because the ill-informed authorities told them to stay put. That feels like a complete betrayal.

Among the victims were two young Italian architects, Marco and Gloria, who lived on the twenty-third floor. They knew about the fire early but were confident that the emergency services would soon extinguish the flames. They waited in their flat. According to one newspaper story, at 2 a.m. Marco spoke on the phone to Gloria's parents in Italy, reassuring them that 'the firefighters are here; everything is okay'. According to a firefighter's unofficial eyewitness account, a team was indeed sent up to the thirty-third floor. But limited oxygen permitted them only to reach the twentieth, where they found someone else to rescue. Marco and Gloria waited for the acrid smoke to diminish. It did not.

By 3 a.m. they knew they were trapped. At 4.07, as flames broke through the walls into their flat, Gloria called her parents for the last time: 'I am so sorry I can never hug you again,' she said. 'I had my whole life ahead of me. It's not fair. I don't want to die. I wanted to help you, to thank you for all you did for me. I am about to go to heaven, I will help you from there.'

Those words haunt me. I'm sure they haunt everybody. They were spoken by a woman who did nothing wrong. She simply followed advice – to stay put.

The pity of it makes me want to run.

The fact is that many more people could have escaped from that building, had they been told to do so. It would not have been easy. There would have been panic. There would have been confusion and choking. Firefighters who removed their breathing apparatus to save some of the victims were themselves injured by the thick smoke. But one young man managed to carry his disabled mother all the way down from the twenty-fourth floor and saved her life.

That is what makes me want to run more than anything else: the thought that it could have been so different. It leads to a fury in my muscles that is also a physical sympathy for the distressed and bereaved. It cannot be wiped away with words.

So I put on my running clothes and simply start running. It doesn't matter how fast or slow I am, or how far or where I go. It doesn't matter that I can feel the stress fracture in my left thigh. The pain is manageable. All that matters to me at this moment is that the physical effort is enough to clear my mind of the stories of smoke and flames, screaming and fallen flashlights – and of Gloria's last words.

I feel so lucky. I have a wonderful sense of freedom. This appreciation of opportunity and hope is as beautiful as the sun rising. Running is such a life-affirming thing. It is a way of finding peace and rinsing ourselves of our worries when the awfulness of mankind's frail state seems just too much. And at the same time, it is reassuring, for when I finish my run, and am lying down on the grass, recovering my breath, I am aware that I have just done the one thing that everyone in that building on that terrible night would have wanted to do.

Run.

21 | OPTIMISM

25 June

Two days ago I was visited by Jonathan Camp – my friend who ran the Bath half marathon with me. We went to the pub. Over a beer, he asked me about my injury. I told him that I'd just started running again. I'd done the run after the Grenfell disaster and was planning to do my first parkrun for 6 weeks the following morning.

'What about after that – are you going to run another half marathon?'

'Of course. I've resolved to do five this year. Another three to go.'

'How long do you think it will be before you're ready?'

I look at my watch. 'Thirty-four hours.'

He spluttered into his pint. 'Do you think that's a good idea? What if you injure yourself again? Why not start more gently?'

'There's got to be some pay-off from my misfortune in getting two stress fractures in the space of eight months. And that, I feel, is the challenge of seeing if I can run the Torbay half marathon from cold. Without any training.'

'Well, all I can say is you're an idiot. You could do yourself some real damage.'

'That's what Sophie says.'

'Don't you think she might be right?'

'Of course. She's always right. It's only my stupid decision to run a marathon in the first place that got me into this predicament. But that doesn't mean I have to *accept* that she's right.'

'You ought to take things easier, do a few parkruns and 10Ks before another half marathon.'

'No, no. This is a physical adventure. I'm taking my body exploring. We're going to places we've not been before. And exploring is just the best thing in the world.'

'Okay, then, if you're going to be like that, I'm going to come along to watch. And if you finish in under two hours I'll buy you a beer.'

When I arrive at Paignton, there is a cold breeze on the seafront. I don't feel comfortable in it. I wish it would die down. As the crowds gather I chat to a fellow runner. Someone dressed as a giant seagull saunters past us and I stop mid-sentence. I don't envy him having to run 13 miles in a 7-foot-tall padded costume. Especially as there is a 3-hour time limit to the race.

There is a countdown to the start over the public address system, and then 1,694 of us are off, jogging along in a mass of colour. I'm in the middle of the pack, taking it very easy. All goes well for the first half of the race. But then we come to a hill and my pace drops dramatically. It is at that point that I realise how unfit I am. I must seriously think about how I manage my energy. Especially because it is growing hotter. Thankfully I feel that beautiful breeze that I cursed earlier.

I am not the only one flagging. Here and there a runner starts to walk, especially on the hills. When someone with a club vest, such as Dursley Running Club, or Storm Plymouth, grinds to a halt and starts walking, other competitors shout, 'Keep going, Dursley', or 'Don't give up now, Storm'. Many are wearing charity shirts that exhort the public to text a certain number to give money. The people who line the streets are clapping and handing out jelly babies. Friends yell encouragement when they catch sight of one another.

Then I hear a spectator shout, 'Go on, Big Bird!'

I glance to my right. The man in the giant seagull costume is running alongside me.

No! Damn it, I am not going to be beaten by a giant seagull.

I speed up slightly.

He stays with me.

Side by side we plod along, Big Bird and I. Everyone cheers him. And I mean *everyone*. This is ridiculous. Although I am very, very tired, and looking forward to the end, I decide that it is worth investing some of my remaining energy for the sake of self-respect. At the next hill, we ascend halfway together and then I sprint for the top. On the descent, all I can do is plod wearily. I dare not look over my shoulder for fear of seeing a large beak. And this is where the running gets unbelievably hard – in the sense that I *need* to stop like an addict needs his next fix. But there is no point in walking now. And I want to be able to say I ran the whole way. In fact, I might even manage to make it in under 2 hours. Jonathan did say he'd buy me a beer... The thought of him waiting at the finish line spurs me on and I struggle up the last slope and down the far side.

I keep going. I'm about 600 metres from the finish line. Ahead of me there is a man lying flat on his back, surrounded by paramedics and helpers. An emergency vehicle and an ambulance are there already. About ten people are helping. Poor guy. I bet he didn't see his race finishing like this. Sometimes you are over-optimistic and put yourself through too much. For my part, I am utterly exhausted. It is all I can do to keep going. But I'm almost there. At last, with the finishing line in sight, and with crowds on either side clapping and cheering, I know I can sprint. The official timing clock says 1:59:21. I am going to make it. I cross the line 25 seconds later.

Jonathan comes over and congratulates me. We walk over to the grass and I lie down. I can't talk yet.

'That was dramatic,' he says. 'The public address system announced that there were only two minutes to go for runners to break two hours. Then it was only a minute, then thirty seconds – and that's when you appeared, tearing down the finishing straight. You must have really wanted that beer.'

———————

As I drive home from Torbay, so the whole picture becomes more coherent – just as the shape of a mountain becomes clearer as you move away from it.

The keyword is 'optimism'.

Why do amateur runners start running again before their injuries have properly healed? Because they are over-optimistic. Why did I think I could run a half marathon without doing any training? Partly because I wanted to see if I could and partly because of my optimism. Optimism seems to pervade everything to do with this sport. Everyone who starts a race is optimistic that they will finish it – even the 8 per cent of runners who did not on this occasion. People are optimistic that by having messages printed on their shirts, others will donate to their good causes. Even people shouting to their friends are optimistic in a way – that their words of encouragement will make a difference.

So much optimism, in every direction. And yet, for most of us who are over the age of thirty-five and declining in strength, running should be exactly the opposite. An arena of pessimism. We're most of us getting slower, and we're all finding it harder by the year. And yet the entire activity turns us into bright-eyed, cheering, bushy-tailed optimists.

Why? Is it that running brings out our optimistic side? Or is it that it eliminates our pessimism?

There is undoubtedly a self-selection principle at work. Some people never run, and that's that. But for the rest of us, when we consider running, we confront a set of stark realities – the distance, our age, our physical condition and a target – and we focus on achieving something despite our acknowledged disadvantages. That focus is essentially what eliminates the negative. We lose sight of the reasons for pessimism – there is no such thing as a pessimistic runner. Then there's the relativism: there's no reason why a running career should be seen as a continual decline if, for example, you measure your performance according to age grades. No one starts running in order to get physically *less* fit. Everyone runs in order to maintain a level of fitness or to improve it. In short, you may not think of yourself as an optimist but if you run, you are an embodiment of optimism, and that's pretty much the same thing.

On top of that, I suspect that running *does* make us more optimistic. It sets us achievable challenges that we would not otherwise face, and thereby creates more opportunities for us to spend time in pursuit of modest successes rather than simply watching television or doing nothing. In that way it gives us what I previously have referred to as 'emotional income'. It also keeps our minds active and alert by giving us physical adventures. If life at fifty appears to be 'a long straight road with death at the end of it' (as a friend of mine once described it), running gives us many opportunities to take turnings off that road – to make the route to death both longer and less straight, and thus the end less obvious. And I think all these things keep us refreshingly innocent and curious: innocent of just how much lies ahead, and curious to see just how many further rewards and pleasures life has in store.

22 | THE TRUEST INHERITANCE

1 July

I am not going to pretend that running a half marathon on a still-not-quite-healed fractured femur was a brilliant idea. The day afterwards it hurt with every walking step. However, being me, I was unable to accept such a tediously predictable turn of events. I grumbled about it for 3 days, after which I decided that I had had enough of my mutinous lower limbs and I was going for a run whether they liked it or not. I lasted 1.61 miles before the pain brought me to a shuddering halt. I walked home in a state of mind that was all of the following: sad, bewildered, weakened, frustrated, lonely, upset, humble and contrite.

As I sat at home the following day, watching the rain pour across Dartmoor, I reflected on this whole business of ageing. I had always thought of growing old as a sort of gradual slowing up. One year you can run 5K in 21:20, the next year it's 21:30, then 21:40 and so on. That's what the graphs say. But that is not how it really is. Instead, you run 21:20 quite happily, year in, year out, and then something suddenly happens that stops you running altogether, and afterwards you struggle to get back to your old fitness. But you never quite make it. The best you will ever achieve in this new world is 21:50, and you have to work damned hard to get back to that level. This model of ageing is not so much a gentle decline as a series of small cliff falls. And each one diminishes our ability to recover.

Today we are heading to Killerton. It is a beautiful morning. The parkland is ecstatic with unfurling fronds of bracken, bright leaves, lush grass and other greenery as we walk up the hill. I notice the old house is covered with scaffolding. It turns out the roof is leaking and needs to be replaced. It too fits my 'series of cliff falls' model of ageing. After so many years, something suddenly gives way, and work is required to keep the structure intact. But no amount of work can ever turn back the clock. Piece by piece, the house crumbles away, becoming an increasing proportion of repair jobs until all you are left with is the bones of the building and a welter of patching that preserves a semblance of its original architecture.

The run director makes his announcement, which unusually includes a 'beware of cows' warning, and then we are off, three hundred of us scampering over the wide expanse of grass. After half a mile, eight or nine bullocks charge across our path. You can tell that most of the runners in front of me are town boys as they stop suddenly, or run away from the animals. I run straight on among them – the bullocks, that is – knowing that they will be far more frightened of me than I of them. Thus I gain half a dozen places. This run is going quite well, all things being considered. Then people start to overtake me again. Among them is Maggie Hunt, the regular 85-per-cent-age-grade lady. *Ah, if I can just stay close to her, I'll be doing okay.* But on the steep downhill section, I twist my ankle badly. I flounder – arms swinging like an intoxicated gibbon's – and hobble for several paces. I tentatively start to run again but, by the time I do, swift Maggie is at least a hundred metres ahead. I grit my teeth and press on. But I am slowing. People are passing me in greater numbers. I see 22 minutes tick by as I run across the grass in front of the old house. *Ageing is not a series of cliff falls or a gradual decline, it is both of those things. That roof was no doubt decaying for decades before it suddenly gave way. You too have been growing slower for years before your stress fractures laid you low.*

I have given it my all. I lie on the grass for a couple of minutes catching my breath before I go and look for Oliver. Like me, he is more than 90 seconds outside his best. This is my worst finishing time ever at Killerton. It's Oliver's third worst. I suggest we drive into Exeter and go to a cake shop. 'Thanks, Dad,' replies Oliver, in that weary-yet-happy-and-reflective way that must have been how soldiers in the trenches greeted news of a parcel from home.

We eat cream cakes sitting on a bench in a sunny churchyard.

What can you do about ageing, especially if it is a downhill slide *and* a series of cliff falls? Clearly you cannot stop it, nor can you put it off. But nor can you ignore it. This is especially the case for those who are genetically programmed to age in a certain way. My father, for example, would have been eighty-two last Tuesday – but he died at the age of fifty-eight years, two months and ten days. A medical research article I read recently, entitled 'Life expectancy and cause of death in males and females with Fabry Disease', reported that the life expectancy of males with his condition was 58.2 years.[4] Dad was spot on the average, dying after a lifetime of ill health. His blood vessels were choked with deposits of a fatty substance that should have been broken down by an enzyme, alpha-galactosidase A. However, his body could not produce that enzyme. Thus his last fifteen years were characterised by both a general decline and many serious 'cliff falls': multiple strokes, heart problems and renal failure among them. Physically, it could have been even worse. My great-grandfather, Charles Beard, from whom my father inherited Fabry Disease, died at the age of forty-seven.

How we age is surely the truest inheritance we have. You might hear the word 'inheritance' and think of a pot of money or a precious heirloom, or even a title and stately home, but all these things can be lost. An heirloom is easily misplaced or taken by thieves. A pot of money is quickly spent even if it is not squandered. The Killerton estate itself ceased to be an inheritance in 1944, when Sir Thomas Dyke Acland gave it to the National Trust. But how you age is something that will always be with you, until the day you die, whether you like it or not.

I think of my own ageing. Do I have a preponderance to suffer stress fractures? That twisted ankle – was it the consequence of an inherited weakness in the shape of my bone? Either way, my genetic makeup is unchangeable. It was laid down when I was conceived, more than half a century ago. The general slowing up is programmed into me as much as it is into everyone else. Should I not just accept my fate and jog along for the rest of my life?

Hang on a moment. Before we start talking about 'jogging along', how long is 'the rest of my life' likely to be? That too is part of my inheritance. How long did my grandparents live?

An average of eighty-four years.

And my great-grandparents?

Apart from Charles Beard, an average of eighty years.

And what was life expectancy at birth when my great-grandparents were born, in the years 1857–85?

Approximately forty-one years of age.

I am thinking the wrong way. I am focusing on how *much* I am declining rather than how little. Yes, there is a general slowing up as we grow older, but the diminution is not that disastrous – at least, not at fifty. As for my cliff falls, they are merely minor setbacks in the context of the next three decades. *Three decades!* How precious an inheritance is that! Imagine that, at twenty, I'd been given a choice: to inherit a multi-million pound fortune and a life expectancy of another 30 years or no money at all and a life expectancy of at least another 60. At that age, I'd definitely have gone for the money and the 30 years in which to spend it. And how much I would have lost thereby! By now I'd have less than 3 months to live, and these days would be my last with my wife and children. Today might have been my final run with one of my sons. No amount of cash could make up for that.

We don't all inherit large amounts of money, titles or stately homes. But all of us benefit or suffer from a legacy of some sort. For some it is physical beauty or an aptitude for languages, great strength or the ability to run fast. For others it is a debilitating medical condition. In my case, it might just turn out to be longevity. Even if I am wrong, I am grateful for the fact that I am still here at nearly fifty, and looking forward to running many years into the future. I might have run slowly today, and have an ankle that looks like someone's stuck half a tennis ball in my sock, and a femur that hurts every time my leg strikes the ground, but ageing is that much more acceptable when you can run with your son and, afterwards, sit in a churchyard together eating cream cakes.

My father would have loved to have done that with any of his sons, even just once.

23 | STARTING TOO FAST

15 July

This week has felt special. Each morning has rejoiced in bright sunshine, and I've drunk coffee in the garden, and eaten a few strawberries while relaxing on the lawn beneath the trees, listening to the birdsong before setting off for a run. Idyllic. I've run four times. On each occasion I'd collapse on the lawn and, after I'd recovered, I would pick and eat a few more strawberries. They tasted even sweeter after the run.

This morning I'm just having coffee, sitting in my study. All the remaining strawberries were picked for a family dinner last night.

I look up from my mug to see Alexander emerge in the doorway, bleary-eyed. Oliver stumbles down from his bedroom and is equally uncommunicative as he joins us. But once we are in the car, both boys perk up. We talk and laugh all the way to Torbay Velopark. It fills me with great happiness to be heading off to run with my sons in such a good mood. In fact, I don't think I could be more content. It is even better than the tranquil moments in the garden eating strawberries. There is an extra sweetness to doing something with family members that beats everything else.

The whistle goes and a man in red immediately takes the lead. A young lad sprints off after him but fades after just 200 metres. After a third of a mile I am running in about sixteenth or seventeenth place. I hear the sound of shoes that click on the ground like football boots. *Those aren't proper running shoes. They probably belong to some young man who has decided on a whim to get fit.* Then, to my great surprise, Alexander overtakes me in his old sneakers. It is the first time he has ever gone past me and I am thrilled! I have been waiting for ages for this to happen – for one of my sons to pick up the baton, as it were – and here it seems to be happening. Only, not quite. He is not strong enough to make the advantage stick. Gradually over the next 400 metres I catch him up. When I overtake him I shout, 'Well done, Alexander,' and he has the courtesy to reply, 'You too, Dad.'

Many things happen in the course of a run and they are soon forgotten but I know I will always remember this moment. It is just the beginning of a process, a handing over to the next generation. It will no doubt happen again and again, and I will continue to catch him up. But then one day he will prove impossible to catch. Or maybe he'll do what his cousin Tom did at the beginning of the year: wait behind me all the way and sprint past at the end. You could say that that is the best metaphor for how we learn from our elders: we shadow them, constantly learning from their example, until we see them weaken, giving us the opportunity to go past. And then we leave them behind.

Today Alexander went off too fast. It is a mistake I myself have made countless times – most memorably in this year's Bath half marathon. That too has its metaphorical side. You can compare it to those stars who burn bright early in life but can't deal with the consequences of success, or who fade quickly when the initial spark turns into the disappointment of a long-term decline. Or those scholars who are brilliant students but who lack the ability to take their subject in a new direction after they have obtained mastery of it, quickly being overtaken by more original thinkers. From the point of view of being a writer, the whole business of setting out too fast and then failing to meet your aspirations is especially salutary. The beginning of a book is crucial – but so are the middle and the end. In fact, just as with a race, it is often only the end of a story that people remember. Going out too fast is a recipe for disaster, you might say.

At the same time, you might take issue with that conclusion. You could argue, for example, that it is better to burn brightly for a short while than never to burn brightly at all. Alexander might not have beaten me today but he did run his fastest 5K ever. A critic would say he had been over-optimistic in adopting that fast early pace. A commentator who had noted his progress would disagree, pointing out that his optimism was the key to achieving his best time. You are wise to start fast if you want to do well. If you don't, you might not use up all your energy before the end of the race, saving it until it is too late. What's more, in starting slowly you set yourself a harder task.

For example, if you want to run 3 miles at an average pace of 7 minutes per mile, you have set yourself a real challenge if you only run the first mile in 7:30: the next two cannot be slower than 6:45, which means you have to speed up significantly after you have already expended a significant amount of energy. That is a big ask. Thus, logically, you may well think that it is best to put your main effort into the start of a race. That way you are bound to convert the major part of your energy into speed. You might have a struggle finishing but at least that struggle will come at the end, when there's only a short distance left. Of course, if you're running tactically then it's not as simple as that. Leaving yourself with nothing extra in the closing stages of a race is risky, especially if you have a rival right on your shoulder. But in the present context, running fast at the outset is a good way to encourage yourself. When you look at your watch and see you've covered the first half of a 5K faster than ever before, you have a huge boost – so you continue to push on and drag the extra performance out of your rapidly tiring legs.

As we drive home Alexander asks me, 'Dad, how can you run so fast?'

The question takes me by surprise, for I don't think of myself as running fast at all. Many men of my age are much faster than me. I tell him it is about an efficient style – arm movements, the way your feet strike the ground – and such things as your weight, level of fitness, how fast your lungs can absorb oxygen, and your body's ability to delay the production of lactic acid. Then I say, 'But what do you mean? You can run just as fast as me. You showed that today. It is simply a matter of keeping going.'

The truth is that he may already be faster than me over a short distance. If today had been a 100-metre sprint, would I have beaten him? No. Today he went off too fast to win – but not so fast he failed to make his mark.

The lesson lies in his achievement, not his failure. There is nothing necessarily wrong in starting too fast. Yes, you might exhaust yourself. But being positive from the outset is also a path to success.

24 | LIES, DAMNED LIES, AND STATISTICS

29 July

Now that the strawberries have all gone, gooseberries, blackcurrants and redcurrants have become my fruits of the garden. It is wonderful, eating them in the shade of the copper beech, before and after running. How different this place is from the dripping bare twigs and earth-slime of 6 months ago, when we cautiously stepped down to the garage before a parkrun, trying not to slip over, and were unable to see the end of the garden because of the mist. Once it was primeval sludge; now it is like the Garden of Eden.

Life is not all sunshine, exercise and fruit, however. Apart from the task of writing the next book, there is the odd bout of heavy drinking. One evening last week my pirate friend, Andy Gardner, helped me to empty three bottles of wine, one can of lager, most of a bottle of port, a quarter of a litre of rum, and the end of a bottle of whisky. The next morning I jogged up the biggest hill in the neighbourhood to sweat out the results. As I plodded along I wondered whether there was some way of having a hangover-related grading system, a bit like age-grading percentages. Say, if you consume 25 units of alcohol the previous evening, then you can compare yourself to the world-record pace for someone of your age, sex and weight who has also consumed 25 units. True, it wouldn't be straightforward to draw up the graphs. In fact, you'd have to hold a series of athletics meetings at which all the competitors would be required to drink dangerous quantities of wine and spirits the evening prior to competing. But in my brain-addled state, the thought of the Hangover Olympics, populated purely by athletes with cracking headaches and bleary eyes, who can barely run in a straight line, was a cheery one. Maybe some of the Beer Mile aficionados would like to enter? It could be quite a spectacular occasion, especially when it came to the pole vault and high jump. In fact, why wait for the hangover? Take the idea behind the Beer Mile and push it to its logical extremes. The champagne steeplechase. The gin sprint. The rum-and-cider discus. I reckon people would pay good money to watch a bunch of athletes down a bottle of vodka and then attempt to race each other over the 400-metre hurdles.

This week, after an uneventful parkrun in Brighton, I resumed my usual training run. I did a 4-mile route on consecutive days. Monday's time was the best, but I reckoned I could go faster, so on the Thursday I really went for it. Coming back up the hill to Moreton was tough. My heart felt as if it was beating like a cocaine-fuelled octopus playing eight simultaneous games of table tennis. I passed a couple of women out walking and thought, *I wonder if they will find me on the way back on the side of the path, dead of a heart attack.* But still I pushed on. At the end I was just one second faster than I had been on Monday.

The closeness of these times made me look for further data about them. They were along exactly the same route in similar conditions but on close inspection they were very different performances. I started off much faster on the second run, and was 22 seconds up after 2 miles, but then slowed. My heart rate was also radically different. Apparently on Monday, it reached an all-time high. Thursday's maximum was normal – much lower – and *that* was the octopus-playing-table-tennis day. However, my average heart rate was almost the same on both occasions. So the second run was steadier. But it wasn't: I went out harder than before and only weakened in the second half.

When the numbers leave you in such confusion, it is tempting simply to repeat Mark Twain's famous quip that there are three kinds of falsehood: 'lies, damned lies, and statistics'. But I was unhappy with the numbers not making sense. So I clicked on a website called 'World Fitness Level' (http://www.worldfitnesslevel.org). This is run by the Cardiac Exercise Research Group of the Norwegian University of Science and Technology. These academics studied peak oxygen uptake in a total of 4,631 Norwegians aged between twenty and ninety. In each case they calculated the maximum volume of oxygen uptake per kilogram of body weight per minute (mL/kg/min), a measurement known as VO_2 Max. Clearly this was more than just your usual online calculator, so I answered their questions to determine my level of fitness. These included my sex, age, height, weight, maximum heart rate, how often and how hard I exercise (which were mere approximations), my waistline measurement, and my resting pulse. The result was as follows:

So, the truth of the matter is: you are forty-nine years old and your expected fitness level is 44 VO_2 Max. However, you have the fitness of an average under-twenty-year-old, and your actual fitness level is 56 VO_2 Max. Keep on going! Your fitness level is good for your age and gender. This means that your heart's capacity to transport oxygen is good, which decreases the risk of dying prematurely from lifestyle-related diseases.

That all sounded wonderful. I especially appreciated the resistance to 'lifestyle-related diseases' in the wake of my drinking bout with Andy. I shouldn't have been so worried about my heart giving out on the cycle path. But in reality the Norwegians' estimate is based on just a few facts. In marked contrast, my Garmin watch puts my current VO_2 Max at 50 mL/kg/min. But how accurate is my watch? In a world riddled with statistics, whose figures do you trust?

I am inclined to trust my watch more than the 4,631 Norwegians. This is not because I have anything against Norwegians; it is due to my actual performances. With a VO_2 Max of 50 mL/kg/min, a forty-nine-year-old man should be able to run 5K on the flat in 19:56, after the appropriate training. This seems about right: if I were to achieve 100 per cent fitness again, that would be my best from last year plus 9 seconds, which is exactly what I'd expect. A VO_2 Max of 56 mL/kg/min, on the other hand, suggests I should be able to run it in 18:05. *Ha, ha; very funny.* Therefore, in considering which data I trust, the experts' calculator comes a poor second to my watch.

This reflection undermines my confidence in the Norwegians' more general conclusions. I am not as fit as someone under twenty. The authors of that study may not be telling ordinary lies, let alone damned ones, but they may well have made a mistake. So might my watch. Either way, I need to err on the side of caution. I need to go back to worrying about whether I'll be found at the side of the cycle path, hand clutched across my breast, gasping with my last breath, 'Don't... trust... the Norwegians.'

Statistics are not lies *per se* but they are fickle, elusive, slippery, hazy, often misleading and frequently undependable. While I stand by my statement in chapter eight that we know something much more completely when we can quantify it, some quantifications relate to things we do not wholly grasp, or are based on misleading or erroneous data. They might help you to understand something, and they *might* tell you exactly what you want to know, but they do not amount to understanding, at least not in themselves. In that respect they're like a beauty spot marked on a map. They guide you in the right direction. But when you have reached the desired place, the best thing you can do is to put the map down. Forget about it. You are missing the point altogether if you make your way to a beauty spot and look at the map and not the view.

25 | HOW FAR CAN YOU DREAM?

6 August

The family is spending a couple of weeks in the south of France, in an old farmhouse near the village of Monestiés, about an hour and a half from Toulouse. Ironically this means everyone else is doing much the same thing as me: quietly reading or writing, drinking wine and eating fruit. I look out across the garden and reflect on the fact that I've exchanged my gooseberries and redcurrants back home for the plums, grapes and pears in the garden here. Figs also grow abundantly and a few of them are just ripening. There is a swimming pool. And it is normally at least 35 degrees centigrade in the early afternoon. If I want to go for a run, I have to set off before 9 a.m. After that it is just too hot.

All the runners in the family are keen to do a French parkrun. The only problem is that there are so few opportunities. For some reason, the French just haven't taken to parkrun in the way that the British and Irish have. At the time of writing there are just nine parkruns in the whole of France, and one of those is suspended due to a lack of volunteers. Also, the French parkruns are not well attended. The two in Paris rarely attract more than 70 runners between them. There have been some French parkruns at which only one or two people have taken part. Compared to the 1,000-plus runners who attend Bushy parkrun in London each week, it's hardly culturally noticeable south of the Channel.

I find this quite intriguing. Athletics is the world's most universal sport, with the sole possible exception of football. Why has parkrun been so phenomenally successful in the UK and yet failed to find fertile ground in certain other European countries? There is not yet a single run in Spain or Portugal, for example. There are none in Belgium, Holland, the Baltic States, Hungary or Romania. Some countries have a few parkruns as a result of local enthusiasts proselytising: Italy has five, Denmark seven and Sweden three. Norway will get its first parkrun later this month. Germany will join the club later this year. Yet there are already 44 in Poland and 28 in Russia – 18 of them in Moscow. Further afield there are 231 in Australia, 17 in New Zealand, nine in Canada, two in Singapore, a dozen in the USA and more than a hundred in South Africa. Obviously, the English-speaking parts of the world have proved more welcoming – but the Polish and Russian numbers suggest that there is no great barrier to parkrun flourishing in other countries. So why is France not part of this?

I don't know. But whatever the reason, the nearest event to where we are staying is the parkrun de la Ramée in Toulouse. That's a drive of an hour and a half each way.

The only alternative is Bordeaux, which is twice as far. So Toulouse here we come.

Parkrun de la Ramée takes place beside a lake, across several long straight paths, only one of which is covered in tarmac; the rest are loose gravel or a combination of grass and bare earth. The largest attendance they have ever had here is thirty-four runners; normally they have about fourteen. Nevertheless, quite a few people are here today. We bump into a family from Brighton, wearing parkrun '100' shirts, as soon as we arrive. Then more runners appear. The organisers seem very happy. In the end, 36 of us gather on the starting line – a new attendance record – mostly English people, about half of whom are on holiday and half ex-pats working at the local Airbus factory.

A Frenchman called Jérôme Costinot gives us a *trois-deux-un* countdown and a young man blasts off into the lead. Matt Ellis, who regularly runs here and helps organise the event, is in a safe second. Alexander is in fourth and I follow him as we run along the path overlooking the lake. At one point he starts to pull away from me but I manage to keep up. Another runner in a blue shirt goes past us. I stay close to Alexander, confident that he will begin to tire before long. But this time he hangs on for almost half the run – 1.45 miles – before I can pass him. Shortly after I do, a Frenchman in his sixties runs past me, puffing heavily. It is Jean-Luc Costinot, Jérôme's father. I try to stay at his pace but cannot. I find my own, more acceptable speed and stick at that for the remainder of the run, finishing seventh. Alexander comes in twelfth, almost 2 minutes behind me, and Oliver eighteenth.

At the end, there is a great celebration. Most parkruns in the UK are very friendly occasions but while almost everyone will chat to visiting runners, regulars mostly go for coffee afterwards with people they already know. Here it is different. There is no café nearby so someone has brought coffee and a stack of paper cups. Someone else has brought a cake – now cut into 36 small pieces. One expat is about to return to America and so someone mixes sparkling wine and orange juice and generously hands out a bucks fizz to everyone who wants one. I nip back to the car to collect my camera and when I return I see Alexander smiling with a plastic glass filled with bubbles.

'All parkruns should be like this,' he announces, sipping his drink.

'Absolutely. A free bar at every finish line,' adds another runner nearby.

Perhaps that is what is needed to increase attendances at French parkruns. Wine. In fact, maybe I should suggest that to the parkrun organisers, as a way of enhancing participation? I can see it now: parkrun with wine in France. Parkrun with pizza in Italy. Parkrun and vodka in Russia. Parkrun and a clotted cream tea in Devon...

---

13 August

I am driving once more to Toulouse, early in the morning. Alexander and Oliver are both asleep in the car, so I am left to my own thoughts as I drive. I pass a herd of cows standing in a field, looking at the only view they will ever know until the day they are taken away to be slaughtered. I look at them and think how lucky I am to have such far horizons by comparison with them. And then the following question just pops into my head:

How far can you dream?

Wow, what do you do with a phrase like that? Turn it into a poem? A song? A life-enhancing speech?

Moments like this, when you have a sudden piece of inspiration, feel magical. Everything suddenly seems possible. It is a sort of Midas moment: every view is golden.

I look down from the hill road on the ancient city of Albi, with its immense thirteenth-century brick cathedral, beneath the pink and pale-blue sky. The clouds have sunk right down into the valleys, so the whole city seems to be emerging from a blanket of mist. For a moment I see the clouds as so much softness, sadness and emotion lining the places where people sleep, and look at the cathedral rising hard and clear above them in the early morning sunlight, like a beacon of timeless philosophy and spiritual rigour. I'm not religious myself but I find medieval churches inspirational. It is incredible that such buildings could be built so well and so beautifully that they would not just stand for 700 years but be the cause of wonderment even in an age that was not beholden to the same spiritual values.

How far can I dream? Not as far as the medieval visionaries who planned this great building. They could see their dream lasting for centuries – forever, even.

I glance at my sons; their eyes are still closed. I drive on in silence.

Place names grab me. Lavaur. Graulhet, Gaillac. Many end in 'ac': Rouffiac, Terssac, Marssac, Loupiac, Grazac... What do they mean? When I am driving in southern England, I normally have a pretty good idea of how the towns and villages gained their names. But here, I could not even tell you how old they are, let alone their origins. All I know is that these places were probably named over a thousand years ago. How distant were the horizons of the people who first described them? How far could *they* dream? Their lives were short, they had no means of transport except small boats, a few horses and perhaps oxen-drawn carts. Yet they travelled a long way in pursuit of their aspirations. We still do today, of course, but it seems a trivial thing to get on a plane to Canada or Australia in pursuit of a job or a better climate, compared to migrating through the unmapped, overgrown and hostile territory of another tribe to find somewhere to bring up a family. The Roman towns around here would have seen the arrival of the Ostrogoths, Visigoths, Vandals, Huns and finally the Franks. How far could they all dream? They were warrior peoples; they didn't build any cathedrals but they crossed whole continents on foot with their children, and they caused empires to fall, with nothing but sharp blades, sharp tongues and a strong self-preservation instinct. They could dream a long, long way – a distance made even greater by knowing the difficulties that lay ahead of them.

Matt Ellis greets us on arrival at the parkrun de la Ramée. The friendly feeling from last week lingers over this beautiful place by the lake, just like the mists hanging in the valleys around Albi. We wait for more people to arrive. More familiar faces turn up. Some visitors too – all greeted with a smile and a handshake, and a conversation about where they are from, and where they usually run. We head to the start and Jérôme takes a picture. Then someone shouts, 'Hold on, there are two more coming.' A man and a woman in their sixties are running towards us, waving. The woman, I note, is wearing a pink shirt and a baseball cap. They are already out of breath before the run has begun. But it is good that they've joined us: the number of runners is now up to 25.

Jérôme holds up the stopwatch. *'Trois, deux, un...'*

Alexander charges straight into the lead. He has woken up at last! There's no way I'm catching him at that pace. Obviously, when he opened his eyes and found he was at a parkrun, he decided that he'd like to be in front for a change. Very soon Matt glides past us, running so efficiently over the gravel that his feet hardly touch the ground. Next, Jean-Luc Costinot overtakes me again and catches up with Alexander. I know from last week's results page that Monsieur Costinot is in his sixties. Neither Alexander nor I has the pace to stay with him, and he impressively pulls away from us both. After about half a mile, Robyn Ellis, Matt's wife, goes past us. And then it is just Alexander and me, in fourth and fifth place, like last week.

Alexander is running strongly. I am still 20 metres behind him when my watch buzzes at the end of my first mile. But I know I can keep up this pace for 3 miles and he cannot. It is only a matter of time. I don't rush. I enjoy the moment. It fills me with pride that he has at last learned how to apply himself. I feel enormously grateful to have such a boy who, at the age of eighteen, wants to come on a run with his dad. I am thrilled that now he is running faster than me. No one told me this sort of thing before I became a father. Isn't it interesting how no one tells you about all the best aspects of fatherhood before the little mite is born? You are expected simply to know them. Or, just maybe, it's more subtle than that. Every other father knows what a delight it will be for you to discover the best things for yourself – and doesn't tell you, on purpose.

We reach the 1.45-mile mark where I caught Alexander last week. I consider a quick sprint to go ahead, but I don't do it. Instead I want to run with him, to encourage him. He is going to shatter his best time for a 5K. I stay behind, willing him on. Back into the woods we turn, back onto another gravel track. Still we are fourth and fifth. 1.76 miles done. I check my watch: the pace is still good. Is he slowing? Yes, but only a little. I put a bit more pressure on and run side by side with him for about 50 metres. Then I go past. 'Well done, Alexander, this is great stuff!' I shout as I overtake.

'Well done you too, Dad,' he replies.

Then he overtakes me again.

My watch buzzes to tell me that 2 miles have passed. This is amazing progress on his part: it's only 4 weeks since he passed me for the first time. On that occasion he stayed ahead for about a third of a mile. The following week he stayed ahead for a whole mile. Last week he stayed ahead for almost a mile and a half. Now he has led me for over 2 miles. At this rate, if I don't speed up, he is going to beat me outright within the next 3 or 4 weeks.

But it is not going to happen today.

I suddenly sprint. 'Bravo, Alexander, brilliant running!' I shout as I go past.

'Go on, Dad, do a PB!'

A few minutes later, I cross the finish line. I am fourth – 45 seconds behind Monsieur Costinot and more than 5 minutes behind Matt, who has run the course in an impressive 16:27. I immediately turn around to look for Alexander. I don't see him straight away because coming in right behind me is a pink vest and a baseball cap. It is the lady in her sixties who had to run to the start. That's an astonishing performance! A sixth runner finishes and then I see Alexander. His time of 22:26 is his best by more than a minute. I throw my arms around him and congratulate him and look back down the long straight for Oliver. He was not feeling that great just before the run. 'Just jog around, take it slow and enjoy it,' I said to him. And that is exactly what he is doing. But he does a good sprint finish at the end.

Back at the farmhouse, I check the results. Although there were only 25 of us running today, there were some very impressive age grades. The lady in pink notched up 88.3 per cent; Matt 82.4 per cent; Monsieur Costinot 77.9 per cent.

Of those three, only Matt is younger than me. It is such an inspiration to see older people running so strongly. It gives me hope for the future.

How far can I dream? I can dream that this will carry on happening for years – that one day I will be one of the old guard overtaking the middle-aged father who is encouraging his eighteen-year-old son, and that one day those fathers will be Alexander and Oliver. I will be then like Monsieur Costinot. I can dream that they will be like him too one day, running with their grandchildren. And this does not just apply to running. I can dream of putting ideas out there that will be discussed in a hundred years' time. It is possible that, in my history books, I can touch the way we think about the past for decades to come – centuries even. In my children, I can impart values that will resonate amongst my descendants and their friends long after my name is forgotten.

Perhaps I am not so different from the men who built Albi Cathedral. I too can dream of creating something that lasts forever.

26 | DESIRE

19 August
Today we have made it as far as my mother's house in Lewes, Sussex. So our parkrun destination this week is Hove Promenade. It will be my seventy-fifth parkrun.

As I drive away from the house, I pass a bus stop and see a young woman standing there. Even though I look at her for no more than 2 seconds – and then only from a distance of 20 or 30 metres – she strikes me as being very beautiful. She is in her twenties, blonde, with a white shirt and black jeans. Her face and her figure exert an undeniable force on me. And probably not only on *me*. There is something primitive, physical and compelling in the way we look and think about members of the desirable sex, and that goes for women as well as men. The newspapers are especially attentive to the desires of millions of female TV viewers transfixed by the semi-naked figure of Aidan Turner, currently starring in *Poldark*. No doubt it is a result of the pre-civilisation phase of our evolution. However much you may think it unbecoming for fifty-year-old men to look at women half their age in this way – however much we ourselves might not want to look at the world through this lens of physical desire because it is socially awkward, politically incorrect and frankly embarrassing – it remains the case that we do. Just as droves of middle-aged women are fascinated by Aidan Turner's bare chest and rippled abdomen.

What has this got to do with running?

Think about it this way. There we all are at the start of a run, wearing next to nothing and waiting, glancing at one another. Then, unexpectedly, you might see a hip or a breast that curves so beautifully that you can only admire how the human body speaks in shapes to the human mind. It makes you feel fully a part of nature, for there is nothing man-made or artificial about such feelings or the curves themselves. When men wear running tights, which ironically are far more revealing than loose-fitting shorts, many of us get to see a physical reaction from other runners. Sometimes you will notice a woman staring at your crotch, sometimes a man. It doesn't matter. It doesn't mean anything – other than that we entice and delight our companions. Such glimpses and glances are just the little compliments that men and women pay each other, every day. Your reaction to an erotic stimulus is as far beyond your control as your need to sneeze. But attraction can be inspirational too. Sometimes I will find myself following a woman dressed in lycra – and her figure will draw me in and encourage me to follow her (just look back to 4 February for evidence…). There is a power simply in being human and letting your instincts take over.

I wonder whether this is true for serious runners too. Surely professionals are above such distractions, single-mindedly pursuing glory to the exclusion of all other passions?

Er, no. Last year there was an article in *The Guardian* about the Rio Olympic Games that began, 'Seventeen days, 10,500 athletes, 33 venues and 450,000 condoms... forty-two per athlete, to be specific.' I don't think anyone would describe me as a prude but 42 condoms in 17 days strikes me as over-provision. It is three times as many as were provided for the London 2012 Olympic Games (*no sex, please, we're British...*). But even that lower number amounts to 14 condoms each over the course of just 17 days (*okay then, not too much sex, please, we're still British...*). And presumably some of the athletes slept with each other, so they only needed one between the two of them on each occasion. Even allowing for a proportion of that huge supply *not* being put to good use, I don't think you can avoid the conclusion that there is a strong link between athleticism and physical desire. The athletes are young and mostly unmarried, they are all living in a restricted-access 'village', surrounded by other people in a similar position, so it's hardly any different from university colleges and halls of residence, which are hardly bastions of celibacy.

Okay, on that basis, here's a hypothesis for you. Those who run fast like to have sex. Those who run really fast *really* want to have sex. Those who can't be bothered to get off the couch simply aren't up for it. Discuss.

Today there are about three hundred runners at Hove Promenade in the sunlit, seaside breeze-ruffled morning.

We are surrounded by keep-fit classes led by instructors wearing either lycra or military camouflage, which strikes me as an odd juxtaposition. People are stretching, jogging and gathering on the promenade to chat prior to the run. No one particularly appeals to my eye, despite the thoughts I have been having on the way here. I look around, just to check. A tanned woman in a blue runner's singlet is talking to a friend but her practical running clothes make her look plain and unattractive. As for the women who are wearing figure-hugging running tights, no one I can see here has the magic line to her body that grabs my animal self within 2 seconds. Having said that, I notice there is a more youthful, vibrant feel to this gathering than at most events. Brighton currently has *four* parkruns, as well as a nudist beach and all these keep-fit classes, so the beauty of the physical body has a far higher priority here than back home in darkest Dartmoor. I try to imagine Moreton having a section of a field set aside for nude sunbathing. Given the amount of rain we get, sunbathing of any sort on Dartmoor would be a pointless exercise. If you were to propose a place be set aside to do it *naked*, your reputation would undoubtedly darken faster than your skin.

The run consists of two laps of the flat tarmac of the promenade. I wish my sons good luck and the whistle goes. Alexander sprints straight to the front and leads the run for about 20 seconds before the fastest runners catch up with him. I stay on his tail, keeping as close to him as I can. At one point he extends the gap between us but by the time we complete our first mile, I am on his shoulder. Then we turn and start running back into the breeze, which suddenly seems stronger than it did before the run.

Despite the wind, this feels like pure running. There are no puddles, no hills, no obstacles. But that very fact makes it psychologically more challenging. Each of the straights is three-quarters of a mile long. There are no twists or turns or changes in the view. The difficulties are rather in your mind, for there is nothing to distract you from thinking *this is uncomfortable*. You are constantly draining your body of energy. Each straight is just as much a battle of wills as running up a hill. Which is why I concentrate on Alexander. After 1.75 miles, I go past him and finish in thirtieth place, 50 seconds ahead. It takes me a while to recover before I can run back to find Oliver. When he finishes he flops down on the grass of the adjacent Hove Lawns. Alexander and I join him.

As we sit there, I see the woman in the blue runner's singlet finish. The perspiration glistens on her collarbone and upper chest in the sun. Strangely, despite everything I said above, she appeals to me much more now than when I saw her earlier. I don't care what she is wearing. Something in our comparably sweating, exhausted states now makes her desirable in my eyes. What we have just been through matters far more than what she is draped in. The sheer physicality of the experience rides roughshod over how pretty or figure-hugging an item of clothing is. I find my reaction surprising because sweating, panting women don't normally do it for me. As she walks away, I reflect that, although she looks nothing like the young woman at the bus stop this morning, the instantaneousness of the physical appeal is just the same, but only *after* she has completed a run.

There is a different dialect here to the language of desire. The nature of what we have just done has changed the character of the signals we send out to each other. In my current state, I see crisp white linen as plain and without substance, merely concealing the real person. It is not the clothes that we are wearing that contribute to our desirability after our run but how vibrant we are. It is as if we see each other's animal states more clearly, and therefore appreciate each other much more physically, and that in turn leads us to notice the points of attractiveness that otherwise we might have missed. Add the sense of relief at the finish, and the euphoria, and you can start to appreciate how a run can spark desire. The unselfconscious glow that follows a race is not unlike that which you feel after making love. Indeed, if you add the elements of fame and fortune that attend the Olympics, you can see why the Olympic Village might need more than a few condom dispensers in the changing rooms.

27 | THE VEGETARIAN'S GIFT OF STEAK

26 August

In past centuries, the year had a ritual quality, being composed of time-honoured and sacred events. First, there were the great feast days of Christmas, Easter and Whitsun, and all the extra religious 'holy days', such as Michaelmas, All Souls' Eve, Shrove Tuesday and Ascension Day. Then there were the other communal landmarks, such as Midsummer's Day (24 June) and Plough Monday (the first Monday after 6 January), when the soil was tilled for the new season. Most of these don't mean as much to us today, even if we do still celebrate them. Instead we have a new set of key dates, such as Valentine's Day, Guy Fawkes Night, New Year's Eve and the final of whichever sporting event interests us most. On top of these, there is the day on which every young person who sits an examination receives the results. Even if you don't have children, you can't avoid the media frenzy that follows Results Day every August. And if you do have children, it is a significant mark on the family calendar.

To cut a long story short, Elizabeth went to her school to pick up her GCSE results and, although she did not do badly, she was disappointed. She passed every subject but was hoping for top marks in some. She didn't get the top grade in any of them.

She rang me up from the school to tell me the news. To be frank, I was quite shocked. I had thought that she would pull a rabbit out of the hat at the last moment. She had assured me she was working hard enough, and I had believed her. But, at the end of the day, we were rabbitless.

As I listened to her on the phone, I did not know what to say.

Situations like this are tough, both for pupils and their parents. It's not the end of the world, true. We've all had disappointments before. But I've been encouraging my children to do well at school since they were very young. I've always told them that academic qualifications are a form of currency that you can carry on spending over and over again, all your life, and they never grow less however much you spend them. I can't turn around now and say to Elizabeth that they don't matter. If she wants to go on to university to study the subject of her choice, which she does, then she needs good grades. It is as simple as that.

The disappointment cast a big cloud over the household. When I went for a run the following day, my heart just wasn't in it. I looked at my watch and saw I was 20 seconds per mile slower than usual. After 3.3 miles I stopped and walked home, disappointed in myself for giving up so easily.

That is when I started to think more deeply about my daughter and her exam results.

Do you not think that she feels disappointed in herself, in just the same way that you are now?

Yes, but there is a difference. It is my choice to run, it is a hobby. Her exams are not a choice. She needs good grades. Next time I will do the full distance but she won't get another chance.

Ian, don't be stupid! Of course she will get another chance. She can make up for this setback, just as you will run this course again in the future. In 2 years' time, she will sit another set of exams, which will render these ones less important. Perhaps this disappointment will prove to be a wake-up call to her? Just as every run carries meaning, even an unsuccessful one like today's, don't you think that her disappointment won't teach her something?

That gave me an idea. As running has taught my sons how to set themselves goals and raise their game, so it could help my daughter. Perhaps I should suggest she come with us? There would be no harm in mentioning it, surely?

On Friday evening, I popped the question over the dinner table. 'Elizabeth, tomorrow the boys and I are going to run at Killerton. What do you think about joining us?'

She looked at me for a moment as if I had just admitted that, prior to her mother kissing me, I had been a frog. In fact, her expression was so severe that I was left thinking I was still a frog. And then she spoke. 'Dad, I am about as likely to go on a run as you are to start eating meat.

You're more likely to run up Mardon, hack a leg off a cow with your penknife and start chewing its raw flesh than I am to go on a run. Do you understand?'

———

It is bright and beautiful in the garden as the boys and I make our way to the car. The blackberries are already ripe, which is surprisingly early for Dartmoor, and I pick a few. I can see that all my walks around the neighbourhood are going to be much slower for the next few weeks as I stop and graze intermittently.

I look up at Elizabeth's bedroom window. The curtains are still closed.

When the run starts, Alexander quickly settles into a steady 6:45 pace, with me on his shoulder. After about a mile, I become aware of a woman behind me: it is Maggie Hunt. She goes past me and draws alongside Alexander. For a few paces I watch the two of them running in front: the 6 foot 5 inch young man with his somewhat gangling movement and the petite woman with her fluent style, so lithe and effortless. Then she passes him. I go with her and overtake him too. He is none too happy to see me in front of him so soon and charges past both of us a few seconds later. Then Maggie and I, side by side, steadily chase him down. After another 300 metres, we pass him. Then I edge in front of Maggie and just manage to stay ahead all the way to the finish. I cross the line 2 seconds before her, then turn and shake her hand, and see her smile. We finish thirty-fourth and thirty-fifth. Best of all, my watch says I am just 3 seconds off my best at this course, 21:21. That is very satisfying.

Alexander finishes in sixtieth place, in a time of 22:50. I congratulate him wholeheartedly. Oliver comes in sight almost 5 minutes later, which is very slow for him. I encourage him nonetheless. 'Great stuff, Oliver! Keep going!' He finishes 172nd, which is his lowest-ever position at Killerton. With each clap of my hands, however, a realisation is sinking in: I am applauding my boys just for taking part. Even though I want them both to be faster than me, it doesn't matter at all that they are not. Yet I did not know what to say to Elizabeth for not being among the best. If you lined up all the sixteen-year-olds in the country according to their overall GCSE results, she would easily be in the top 10 per cent. And what's more, she has achieved this in spite of all the pressure she was under to perform well – pressure for which I was responsible as much as anyone.

As the runners stream in, the shadow of that realisation grows. And it is a dark shadow. I think back to my own childhood and the way I would put my poor parents through the worry mill. I didn't want to have to deal with the pressure of success so I did nothing to prepare for my mock exams. I failed them deliberately so that, when it came to the actual event, there was no weight of expectation. I could relax in the smug knowledge that anything apart from complete disaster would be counted a success. I had all the self-confidence of youth. I was arrogant. My daughter now has to deal with both the weight of expectation *and* having me as a father. Has my arrogance diminished since I was a teenager – or has it simply found another outlet?

I watch more people finish the run, smiling, happy just to do their best.

I have been a hypocrite.

I clap them in, feeling deeply sorry. When Elizabeth phoned me up and told me her results, I should have congratulated her just as warmly as I have just applauded my sons for running – as warmly as I am applauding all these strangers for getting up and jogging around the park.

As we drive away, I want to do something grandiose for Elizabeth – both to celebrate her achievement and to say sorry. Whatever it is, it needs to be special. I must do something that demonstrates that I am proud of what she has done and, at the same time, aware that I should have said more to praise her.

But what?

I think back to last night, and her declaration that I am more likely to eat meat than she is to run. We never cook meat at home, because Alexander and I and several of our friends and relatives don't eat it, and Sophie is adamant that she won't cook it when we are in the house, out of respect for us. Besides, it is easier to manage the family larder and cooking utensils on a completely non-meat basis. But Elizabeth's favourite food is steak.

It might seem odd for a non-meat-eater to choose to 'say something' with steak but on the way home I make a detour to a supermarket and buy steak for her and the other meat eaters in the family. I hope this evening she realises I am not just saying 'sorry'; I am also saying I am proud of her. I can see now I should have realised this all along, for it is what all parents should bear in mind when a son or daughter faces a significant challenge. But sometimes you need something like running to remind you.

I love my daughter for who she is, not for what I hope she will be.

28 | BENEVOLENT COMPETITIVENESS

9 September

You might remember that one of my New Year's resolutions was to play a game of chess against Oliver every week: a grand match of 52 games. At first, things were neck and neck – never more than a couple of games in it – and the advantage was normally with me. However, when we went to France, Oliver stormed into the lead. Now he is five games ahead, 19 to 14. The thirtieth game was especially impressive: I was a castle up and sure of victory but he completely outplayed me. What is different is his confidence. Earlier in the year he *tried* to beat me, and sometimes did so. Now he doesn't need to try. It looks as if he is overtaking me mentally at just the same time as Alexander is catching up with me physically. It is curious: I am as competitive as ever but not at all disappointed – quite the opposite. It is not simply because it is 'meant to be that way'; rather it feels that their triumphs are my triumphs. Indeed, one of the greatest joys of fatherhood is being able to compete with your children as hard as you can and then take pride in their victories.

When I was a boy, I didn't understand this. I could not see the relationship with my father from his point of view. Nor did we compete. He did not play chess, nor could he run. He was an architect and a very practical man but not remotely literary or academic. Only once did we ever race each other. It was when I was about ten or eleven years of age. We came across a running track while out walking, and I challenged him to a lap. I overtook him after about 200 metres and he gave up. An old man watching came over to us afterwards and said to my father, 'This is when you know you're getting old.' I did not appreciate then that he was probably happy to be beaten by me. It signalled my achievement, not his failure. Through raising me, my success was his success too.

This sense of benevolent competitiveness is one that I don't hear mentioned in public discourse. Recently there was a programme on BBC Radio Four in which women were talking about competitive sport. Some had clearly been left deeply scarred by their experiences at school. Others were against competition for other reasons, such as the possibility that it encourages an adversarial approach to society. A few women spoke up for the opposite point of view – that women can be just as competitive as men, and can benefit accordingly – but generally there seemed to be a feeling that, when it came to exercise, women and girls should stick to 'dance, yoga, long-distance walking (with or without a dog) and casual swimming'. I was dismayed. To avoid competition is to deprive yourself of the many opportunities that we enjoy when we do sport together, surely? Also, if you want to see more women in Parliament or in business, you need to encourage not only the ability to compete but the desire to do so. But what really struck me about the whole discussion was the fact that no one even mentioned the benevolent form of competitiveness that I described above. No one is going to try harder than Alexander to beat me in a race, and when he does, I will be proud of him, just as I am proud of Oliver for taking a commanding lead in our chess games. Their triumphs are my triumphs.

The question is, will Alexander beat me today? Indeed, so rapid has been his improvement that I cannot hope to stay ahead of him much longer. In the first quarter of this year his parkrun speed was 86 per cent of mine. In the second quarter, it increased to 89 per cent. But over the last 2 months his speed has averaged 93 per cent of mine and twice he has exceeded 96 per cent. If he continues to get faster at this rate, he will easily beat me by the end of the year.

He smiles when I tell him this. 'Challenge accepted,' he says.

───────────

I am making coffee when Alexander comes into the kitchen. We chat for a while, mainly about his old school friend, Alfie Fell, who is going to join us today for a parkrun at Parke. Alfie is one of those excessively talented boys who is not only outstandingly academic but excellent on the sports field and even more impressive as a musician. I really don't have much hope of outrunning him.

Oliver has overslept. I wake him with about 20 minutes to go. When he comes downstairs, he is still a little bleary-eyed and just listens to us talking. Then he suddenly interrupts. 'Hold on a minute,' he says to Alexander. 'When you were at primary school, didn't Alfie beat you in the cross-country?'

'He did. He came first, I came fourth,' replies Alexander.

'Was that the race when you cried?' presses Oliver mischievously.

I laugh. 'It was. I remember it well.'

'Da-ad,' moans Alexander.

'So then,' Oliver goes on, smiling at his brother, 'if he beats you today, are you going to cry again?'

'Probably,' Alexander answers, laughing.

The ground is sodden after 2 days of rain. As I drive to Parke, I can see it is going to be 'proper muxy', as an old Devon-dialect speaker would say. When the whistle goes, Alexander runs off fast, in about eighth position, hotly pursued by Alfie. I can't keep up with them and watch them get further and further away as we descend to the gate. Then, as we ascend the 1-in-4 hill, they increase the gap. I plod on, in about thirtieth position. I feel heavy and unused to running. My feet sink into the mud as if they want to sleep there. Unsurprisingly my watch shows my first mile is slow. But I keep going at the same steady pace. And after another third of a mile, I see Alfie and Alexander just 40 metres ahead. Alfie is staying on Alexander's shoulder. The gap shrinks: 30 metres, 20, 10. I see my chance. I wait until there is clear space to pass them both and then I go for it. But Alexander has recognised the pattern of my breathing and, without turning around, knows that I am there. He sprints ahead. Alfie goes with him. Keeping on the pressure, I pursue them over the stones and mud of the track, splashing through the deepest puddles. Alexander only lasts a few seconds more and then I pass him convincingly. But Alfie comes with me. I can hear his soft footfall but otherwise he is silent. I can't even hear him breathing. He is running almost effortlessly, just biding his time.

When we reach the path along the disused railway line, I am feeling tired. I struggle to the foot of the second hill and pace myself up it, taking smaller steps. Alfie stays behind me for about 5 seconds and then sprints up the slope. By the time I am at the top he is 20 metres ahead, chasing down a man in a lime-green top.

I smile as I watch him go. I have known him since his first days at school. I watched him as a little boy smartly march out of the school gate in his uniform to greet his waiting parents, and I've seen him in torn jeans head off with Alexander to build tree houses and camps in the wooded valley north of Moreton. I've watched him amaze people of all ages with his sweeping guitar technique at the Battle of the Bands, when as fifteen-year-olds, he and Alexander took their heavy rock onstage. And now here he is, at eighteen, running off into the distance. When I finally make it to the finish line, covered in mud, I am more than a minute behind him.

The lesson of all this for me is that benevolent competitiveness is not just a matter of parents and children, for I felt it too with regard to Alfie. I was happy to see him go ahead of me. That makes me wonder whether all competitiveness in this sport is in some way 'benevolent'. Just as the desire to compete itself is a matter of degrees, and not simply a black-and-white contrast, so too we might think of any runner's performance on a spectrum from disinterest to benevolence. Indeed, is an amateur sport competitive at all? I can applaud family members and their friends beating me, and older people showing their mettle and passing me, and young boys and girls overtaking me, and women of my own age who persevere and get past, and so on. Is it being competitive, if I don't mind being beaten? I conclude it is not.

When I see someone playing guitar better than me, I am not unhappy – quite the opposite. Likewise when they run faster than me. I am pleased to watch fast runners show how talented they are, and thrilled to see young people do something better than I can. It is not a matter of competitiveness but appreciation.

As I am writing the above paragraph, however, I am interrupted by a shout at the back door. Nicky Hodges, a charismatic (some would say 'eccentric') retired GP and a good friend has let himself in and wants to have a chat. He sees me at my desk, still in my running kit, covered in mud.

'You've been running.'

'I have, Nicky. Parkrun.'

'Don't see any point in it myself. Why bother? All that effort.'

'But it is such a powerful common denominator. It gives me so many ideas – so many things to write about.'

'Like what? Left, right; left, right; left, right – end of chapter one. Start of chapter two: left, right; left, right; left, right… Can't wait to read chapter three.'

'Nicky, in the same way that good writing is more than just a succession of words, so running is more than a mere sequence of steps. Today, for example, I watched Alfie Fell run ahead and beat me, despite my best efforts. And it gave me a deep sense of satisfaction.'

'It means nothing to me, all this competitiveness.'

'But it is not competitive.'

'Yes, it is, by your own admission. You just used the word "beat". If that is not a sign of competitiveness, I don't know what is.'

'But it's not the sort of competitiveness that makes someone feel second-best, or belittles anyone's achievement. Amateur running lifts everyone up, even those at the back of the pack, who can at least find satisfaction in the fact they are improving their health.'

'Bollocks! Improving their health? Have I told you about my favourite cartoon? It shows two runners on a track: one is lying dead, and the other is looking down on him, saying, "What a way to go! At the very peak of fitness."'

'You can't argue that running is not good for you. You are a medical man.'

'Look, in thirteen days' time, you'll turn fifty. In eleven days' time, I'll be seventy-five. And I've never even run for a bus. If you get to seventy-five, it will be in spite of your running, not because of it.'

After he has gone, I reflect on his comment on my use of words that are, to him, clear signs of competitiveness. I suppose he is right. My shades of competitiveness are still a matter of one person beating another, however benevolent one may feel. The difference between me and the anti-competitive women on the BBC Radio 4 programme is that I like competitiveness because I see it as bringing people together and helping them fulfil their potential, whereas the women see it as threatening. Some of them fear it forces people to confront their inadequacies in front of others, to the extent they feel humiliated. The question is why? How does someone end up feeling this way? Why can't all competitiveness be benevolent?

I reckon the answer to that question is that we encounter competitiveness at a far earlier stage of life than we do benevolence. We lack the maturity and the confidence in ourselves to wish all our schoolfriends well. Especially the bullies. Yes, there are some people I remember whom I would never have been happy to see pass me. I would have wanted anyone and everyone to beat them.

All of which leads me to the conclusion that there are three forms of luck in this world. There's the luck of born winners, like Alfie, who just excel at something naturally. Then there's the luck of those who do not need to compete, like Nicky, who reach the age of seventy-five without ever having had to 'run for a bus'. And then there's the luck of people like me, who are forced to compete and initially hate it but who manage to turn things around and, over the years, come to love competitiveness through recognising the embrace it offers, and who appreciate the excellence of others and can share in their joy when they do well.

Frankly, I think people who fall into the third category are the luckiest of all.

29 | THE GENTLEMEN'S TRIATHLON

16 September

The idea occurred to me while swimming in the pool in France. I was gently coming to the end of a length of breaststroke and it struck me there ought to be a triathlon that is all about enjoyment, not speed. In this, you would do your 1,500-metre swim, 40-kilometre bike ride and 10-kilometre run – but you would do them slowly. You would not be allowed to finish in *less* than a certain time. I considered this for a moment and then realised what a stupid idea it was. If someone wants to do a triathlon slowly, he or she can – he doesn't need to stop other people from doing it fast. So, as I swam back, doing my lazy backstroke, I thought harder. *Why isn't swimming included in a decathlon? It's one of the most important physical tests.* And then as I did another length of breaststroke, I pondered the idea of a varied test. *Why is there no intellectual test in a decathlon or a triathlon – why are they only concerned with physical feats?* And then the idea hit me. What about holding a gentlemen's triathlon, a sort of duel, in which there is a physical challenge (a run), a mental sparring (a game of chess) and a test of dexterity (a racquet sport). That would surely be the ultimate competition.

Immediately my thoughts went to Andy Gardner. Back in February he accepted my challenge to do a parkrun later this year, in a drunken moment of camaraderie which he hoped in vain that I would forget. He can play chess too – the last time we played, he beat me. On the other hand, when it comes to table tennis, we are more or less even. I challenged him to a 'gentlemen's triathlon', as I called it. He graciously accepted.

It takes place this Saturday.

_____

It is a beautiful morning, the sun glinting across the moor in the distance, and the coolness of early autumnal wistfulness in the air. Beads of dew hang from the branches of plants in the garden. The ground is very wet, as it's rained every day this week, so even though we'll be running on the flat, at Torbay Velodrome parkrun, the times won't be fast. *That doesn't matter. Today isn't about speed, it is about the competition between us.* Except that that's not true. I still want to get back to a higher level of fitness, running 20-minute parkruns in my fifties. Therefore I set myself the target of 13 minutes for the first 2 miles, which are almost entirely run on the track. That will mark progress.

An average time of 6:30 per mile equates to a total time of 20:11, and that would be a significant improvement on my best time over the distance so far this year.

Oliver, Elizabeth and I are waiting in the kitchen when we hear the clang of the gate. Oliver and I are dressed for running but Elizabeth is still in her dressing gown.

'Aren't you joining us?' Andy asks her jovially.

'Nah, not my thing,' she says, all smiles.

Now, if I had asked her that question, I would not have got off so lightly. How different are the faces we present to the world outside the family! It makes me feel privileged for a moment: that she reserves her real thoughts on the subject of running, with all their splenetic fury, for me.

Andy is normally very confident in everything he does. He is the sort of man who can go into a pub and start singing an old folk song – and everyone quickly falls silent, listening. It is not so much that he has a great voice, it is rather that he has terrific presence and the confidence to be very expressive in a crowd of strangers. Thus, when we get to the start of the run, it amuses me to see him out of his comfort zone, uncertain where to place himself. There are well over two-hundred runners here – 262 it later turns out – from lean young men and women to older, experienced hands, and heavier, out-for-a-jog-and-a-chat participants. He looks around and initially lines up next to Oliver. Then I catch his eye: I know what he is thinking. He is a few years younger than me: if *I* can be bold enough to stand at the front, so he should too. He steps forward through the crowd. 'No point giving you the advantage of a few metres,' he announces, slapping me on the back.

When the whistle blows he sets off fast. I stay on his shoulder, in about sixth or seventh place. But he cannot keep this pace up and he starts to slow after less than 30 seconds. This is not going to be a contest, I realise, as I sweep past him. At the first bend I glance across and see he has already fallen back by about 80 metres, and Oliver is not that far behind him. So I set my sights on the time challenge – not over-reaching myself but not relaxing too much either. A man overtakes me and I stay with him, adjusting my speed to his: this pulls me along for about 300 metres. Then I overtake him in turn and pull away. A little later a woman in a purple club vest catches me and goes past, and I follow her pace too for some while, until she increases her speed and leaves me. My watch bleeps to tell me my first mile is up: 6:21. *That is good. Now, the next one at the same speed, please.* But, of course, you slow down even though you're putting in just as much effort. I am lucky, however. A young man in a black singlet comes alongside me and provides me with the pace I need. When my watch buzzes for the second time, it reads 6:39. I have hit my target on the nose: 13:00 for the first 2 miles.

The field is indeed as muddy as I thought it would be. Those ahead are spread out over a distance of half a mile. As I run I can hear a woman's light quick breaths behind me – and the knowledge she is there spurs me on. I don't turn around but make sure I stay ahead of her. When we are 200 metres from the line I start to sprint across the pebbles and broken tarmac. She comes with me but cannot overtake before the finishing line. At the end, I immediately turn around to thank her for propelling me on for the last section. She gives me a big smile as she shakes my hand. I check my watch: 21:16.

I run back to see how the others are doing. Oliver appears first, about 3 minutes behind me, steadily keeping up his easy gait. I run with him across the line, urging him on. 'Sprint! Sprint, Oliver, go on! Sprint like you did in France. Come on, it's only another hundred metres.' He blithely ignores me but still finishes in 24:37, which is inside his target time. I embrace him and run back to find Andy. He is a long way back but still going. I run alongside him to the end and feel guilty for persuading him to run. He is absolutely shattered. He can't speak. We walk around so his legs can recover before getting back in the car. It turns out that that is the first time he has run anywhere for more than 20 years. I am impressed that he managed to keep going the whole distance.

About 3 hours later, after coffee, we sit down to play chess. It has started to rain now, so we play on the balcony outside my bedroom, overlooking the moor. I am playing white, and I open with my king's pawn. Andy responds, very slowly. He puts a lot of thought into every move. Normally my games with Oliver are over within 20 minutes but here the intensity is much greater. Andy's concentration forces me also to spend more time thinking, and more possibilities become apparent. Early in the game he brings his queen out aggressively, and I see she is on the same diagonal as my bishop, with two of my own pieces between them. Over the course of the next few moves I take these intervening pieces into play elsewhere, advancing a pawn and moving a knight off that diagonal to attack a crucial bishop. My ploy works! He is distracted and does not notice that his queen has gradually been exposed. I take her. He kicks himself for not seeing the threat. But he is resolute and, boy, there is no way he is giving in. He builds the pressure on my king, especially after I castle. I retaliate by ratcheting up the tension with a bishop-and-queen attack. The game is so intense, it is almost hallucinatory. I am hearing every drop of rain falling on the leaves of the plants and trees in the garden. The birdsong is so clear that, when it is his move, I hear their calls as if they were all perched around my chair, watching. When it is my move, it is as if they all fall silent, waiting to see what I do.

'It doesn't get any better than this,' he says.

It is raining. It is hardly the luxuriant warmth of France. Yet he is right. I would not be anywhere else right now.

Gradually more of his pieces fall to me. He has to make too many concessions. Finally, he is forced to shift a piece that allows me to trap his attacking castle. He knows the game is up and concedes. We've been playing for more than an hour and a half.

After a late lunch, we take our table-tennis bats for the third and final round of the triathlon. He is just as competitive as ever, and determined to win at least one of these contests.

But I don't play badly, and the best-of-seven-games match ends up with me winning 4:2.

At the end of the day, I think about the benefits of rivalry. It was the challenge of competing that made Andy run 5K this morning – something for which, believe it or not, he is grateful, despite the fact that his muscles are now causing him considerable discomfort. Moreover, when I was running, each of those people who tussled with me for the next place helped me along. They were little rivalries, lasting only 30 or 40 seconds in some cases and only a minute or two in the case of the last one. But for those short periods we were bound together in the drive to win or keep that place, and so we encouraged each other to do better.

This does not just apply to running. I sometimes look back across the centuries and see how, when the most prominent exponents of an art or science made their mark, it was frequently after the threshold for success had been raised by a rival, whether a predecessor, teacher or other leading figure. Think of Plato and Aristotle in philosophy, Mozart and Beethoven in music, Turner and Constable in art, Freud and Jung in psychoanalysis. The more you think about it, the more examples you can find. The outpouring of great dramatic writing in London after 1587 was due first to Thomas Kyd and Christopher Marlowe laying down the gauntlet and then to William Shakespeare and Ben Jonson picking it up. In mathematics, Isaac Newton and Gottfried Leibniz almost simultaneously made the breakthrough in developing calculus. Leonardo and Michelangelo were direct rivals in art, practically scoring points off each other as they painted battle scenes in the Palazzo Vecchio in Florence. You can't read more than a few words of Benvenuto Cellini's autobiography and not realise that his career was about proving himself a greater artist than all his contemporaries. In art as well as sport and science, rivalry spurs people on to greater levels of excellence.

This is not just what great artists and scientists do, feeding off each other to produce the pinnacles of human achievement; this is what most of us do in our everyday lives. Am I pushed on by rivalries in the history profession? Of course! When I publish a research article and someone responds, saying they don't accept it for this or that reason, the challenge is laid down – for me to reconsider the argument and, if I feel I am correct, to push it that bit further. Total and complete historical understanding is like running 5K in zero time – impossible – but you can always improve that little bit more, in both endeavours. In history, you can do this by researching extensively, or by reading around the subject and visiting sites in an attempt to understand something more fully. In running, you can do it by training more intensively or changing your diet. As you improve at either task it gets harder and harder to increase performance still further. Eventually you reach a point at which you have read all the major sources for a historical event and then you are into the realms of improving your understanding by questioning received wisdom – and that requires you to analyse and criticise other people's work. With running, the training will only take you so far: most athletes produce their best performances in competition. In both cases, you need the rivalry to push you on – to go further than other people would normally go. In short, you need rivals if you want to recognise your full potential.

At the end of the day, Andy stresses how much he has enjoyed the 'gentlemen's triathlon'. He is the perfect sportsman. I tell him that I am in his debt. Not only did I also enjoy the day, he pushed me on to run well, and to play the best game of chess I have played in a long while. He then says that, now he knows he can run 5K, he wants to do it again – and close the gap on me. He is inspired.

What positive things we can do for one another! We would be a miserable species if we all lived individually in separate burrows and never played together, or worked together, or sang, ran and swam together. All our achievements would lack the social dimension that gives them context and meaning. The fact our rivalry today inspired us both to go that bit further makes me ask, what is the real purpose of rivalry? Forget the idea that it is all about being top dog or the dominant member of a tribe. Rivalry is far more subtle and sophisticated than that. It exists so that people help each other and inspire each other to reach new heights. Ultimately, it serves to remind us that we are stronger together than we are as individuals. Regardless of who wins and who loses, its great virtue is social bonding. Or, as I prefer to think of it, friendship.

30 | IS AGE JUST A NUMBER?

23 September

The last run of my forties was a steady 8.6 miles over the hills above Moreton. On my return, I lay down on the lawn and was welcomed home by one of our cats, Dexter, who came over to nuzzle me. Stroking him, I felt a tremendous sense of nostalgia for that very moment, even as it was slipping by. In truth, of course, it was nostalgia for my forties. Is fifty just a number or does it mark a real change in life and the way I think? Will entering my sixth decade have any effect on me? Is it the high point of being 'middle-aged'? Indeed, is all this running just a facet of a midlife crisis?

My fiftieth birthday was yesterday, a fine day. Although it has nothing to do with running, one moment of serendipity deserves to be recorded. I took the family to the Ritz in London for cocktails. Sitting on a plush sofa, Elizabeth remarked on how she did not feel comfortable in such a grand place. 'It's too posh for me,' she said.

'What do you mean by "too posh"?' I replied.

'Too upper class.'

'Never! Look, last time your mother and I were in here, on our wedding anniversary, Rod Stewart walked in. No one would call him posh or upper class. He was born in north London and went to the local comprehensive school. But he seemed quite at home here. You can get used to such a place. If a lord and lady came in through the front door, you would not know them from Adam and Eve. The lord might well be wearing a suit and would probably have very little hair, like me, and few countesses look as elegant as your mother does today. Would you feel out of place if everyone in here looked like us? It's not about class. Nor is it about fame. It's about how much you want to be here. Do you like the ambience, the décor, the food and the people? Do the staff provide you with what you want? Do they treat you with respect? I'm sure that if you came here regularly, you'd soon feel just as much at home as Rod Stewart.'

At that moment, Sophie said, 'Oh, look!' and burst out laughing.

Rod Stewart had just walked in.

Oliver turned to me. 'He probably thinks you drink in here all the time.'

––––––––––

The alarm goes off, and I have no good idea why. I open my eyes and it dawns on me that I am at my mother's house in Lewes. The alarm says 7 a.m. Then, with an almighty throb in my head, I become aware of the scrapheap behind my eyes. My mind is indeed like so many rusting vehicles with weeds growing through their smashed windows and oil-dripping gearboxes. My thoughts are going nowhere, creaky and unstarting. I can't even bring myself to make a coffee.

Then I remember. At about 2 a.m. last night I told everyone I would drive to Hove Promenade parkrun this morning. *What the hell was I thinking? Oh no! It is coming back to me now.* Just before Alexander and Oliver went off to sleep at my brother's house up the road (where there is more room), I told them that, if they wanted to run, they should meet me at a certain spot at 8.10 a.m. I very much doubt they will be there. *But what if they do turn up and I don't?*

I drink some water and gaze out at the morning mist that lurks beyond the scrapheap.

At 7.55 I leave the house and drive off to Robbie's. I wait outside, sure that no one will be joining me. But after a few minutes the front door opens.

'Ah, you're here,' says Robbie, holding the door open. Oliver follows him out. 'I can't promise you it will be a fast time, but we can't let an old man run on his own.'

———

I start at a moderate pace. It is the best I've felt so far this morning, with the calm sea on my left and the gentlest of breezes on my face. I count the number of runners ahead of me as they turn around a bollard at the end of the long straight: I am in thirty-fifth place. I set myself the task of improving on that and start to close on those ahead. At the third hairpin, I count 32 people ahead of me. I lengthen my stride on the penultimate straight and turn the last hairpin in twenty-ninth. Two men ahead of me are catchable, one far out on the right-hand side of the promenade and the other directly in front of me. *You're still running steadily, so you've still got a sprint in you.* With 300 metres to go, I pass the man in front. *But look – the chap on your right has already started to quicken his pace. Go for it!* I push on hard. He responds. We are side by side for 5 or 6 seconds. Then I push yet harder, and he can't stay with me. I finish twenty-seventh out of 282.

It is only when I look at the day's results on the website that it hits me. My age category now reads 'VM50–54'. I don't identify with that at all. It is like someone telling me I live somewhere far away, in a distant town that I have never visited. Where is that place? Who is that person? Yet the reality is that my quaint and homely VM45–49, where my cat nuzzles me after a run over the hills, is mine no longer.

I have been moved on, forcibly. Evicted by the bailiff of time.

I can't quite understand why this is such a shock. I have been thinking about turning fifty all year, but it is still mildly disturbing. When someone is expected to die for a long while, you get used to the fact that they are dying and so it comes as a surprise when they finally do pass away. It seems much the same with age. I've been anticipating turning fifty for so many months that I find it quite disarming to have passed the milestone. I have become too familiar with the anticipation.

I stare at the results page. Is all this running a symptom of a midlife crisis? Maybe it is. In fact, if entering my sixth decade preoccupies me to this extent, I really have to think of it in those terms. But in accepting this, I also have to consider it alongside all the other 'crisis' moments of my life. You could say that it is not just a 'midlife' phenomenon but another episode of a lifelong one. As a child, I was terrified of infinity, dreaming nightly of a tightrope that rose from the backdoor of my grandmother's house to a great height in the sky. It ran all the way around the world, and I was doomed to have to crawl along it – to tightrope-walk my way around the entire globe. In my late teens, love affairs, examinations, the instinct to rebel, the pressure to conform and the need to develop an identity were just a few of the things that preyed on my mind. Teenage angst reaches deep into the soul, feeding off the childhood nightmares that will always lurk there, like spiders in the dark. Those worries then grow with us over the years into doubts about marriage, money, illnesses, the loss of friends and whether we will ever fulfil our ambitions. Come to think of it, my childhood and teenage crises did not properly diminish until I had children, in my thirties. Then, like any other responsible parent, I had to prioritise the vulnerability of others. That stifled all my personal doubts for a while. Now, becoming fifty is just a gentle reminder that they are still there, those spiders, and may yet emerge from their dark crevices.

The more I stare at the age grouping 'VM50–54', the surer I am that people who are given over to worry will always carry a personal crisis with them. A midlife crisis is just the middle-aged manifestation of this lifelong tendency. In this light, it is not surprising that some men try to tackle it by starting new relationships with younger women. After all, a new family would allow them to suppress their fear of ageing and death by giving them a whole new set of priorities to quell their personal dilemmas. But for the rest of us who have no desire to waltz off with a younger partner, how should we tackle the onset of middle age? Buy a fast car? A motorbike? Quit the day job and travel the world? Or just start running? That last option is surely the least destructive one.

Your age is not just a number – no more than *you* are just a number. Fifty is a significant landmark which should make any intelligent person think deeply about what it means to grow old. It raises questions about your achievements to date and what the future holds. It is the point at which you stop counting up your age in how many birthdays you have passed and start counting down – speculating how long you might have left to live – with a view to leaving a legacy of some sort. But despite my shock at stepping over this border, two things are clear. The first is simply that you'd rather turn fifty that not. We've all lost friends at tragically young ages, who've died knowing they will never fulfil their ambitions or see their children grow up. And second, even if your running *is* just a reaction to your midlife worries, it is a better strategy than rushing off with the young blonde from the bus stop or splashing out on a new sports car. Indeed, if people only discover you are struggling to come to terms with ageing because you have taken up some form of physical exercise, then you are already one step ahead of them. And if some of those newspaper headlines about the benefits of running are to be believed, you may even be one step ahead of the ageing process itself.

31 | PILGRIMAGE

7 October

Today is International Parkrun Day: the day on which the parkrun community commemorates the anniversary of the first parkrun, or the first 'Bushy Park Time Trial', as it was originally called. On 2 October 2004, 13 runners set off – ten of them being friends or acquaintances of Paul Sinton-Hewitt, the man behind the whole project.[5] And out of respect for him and what he has achieved over the subsequent 13 years, I've been planning all year to attend this commemorative event.

The statistics for Bushy Park speak volumes. After that first run, 14 runners turned up for the second time trial, then just 11 for the third. It looked as if it was going to struggle to get off the ground. But 20 turned up the fourth week – and it's grown from there. The first anniversary run, in October 2005, saw 155 people take part. In recent years, it's been common for more than a thousand to attend. On the tenth anniversary, in 2014, no fewer than 1,705 people ran. Last week was the 700th run at Bushy and 1,229 people took part, not including the small army of volunteers. No other parkrun in Britain is so well attended on a regular basis, and that highest-attendance figure has, at the time of writing, only been exceeded by three other parkruns, all in South Africa. In addition, the fastest unassisted parkrun to date anywhere in the world was completed at Bushy on 11 August 2012, when Andrew Baddeley ran it in 13:48. The second-fastest time by a female parkrunner was also recorded here, when Justina Heslop ran 15:58 in 2011 (second in the UK only to Hannah Walker's 15:55 at St Albans in 2013). In terms of history, popularity and performance, you could say it is to amateur running what Wimbledon is to tennis and what Lord's is to cricket.

The real story of Bushy, however, is not the growth in numbers or the speeds achieved but Mr Sinton-Hewitt's inspiration. In a world that is depressingly cynical and critical of others, his philosophy is remarkably uplifting. As he put it:

From day one, I never wanted parkrun to compete with the clubs and I didn't want it to compete with the races. I just wanted to be a part of the community. My objection to clubs and governing bodies is that they feel they own you and they can direct you to do things, and in fact, that's not true. People do what they want to do. All we are doing here is building a playground, and if you want to come and take part, you can. People have recognised that it's free in every sense of the word – it's not just that you don't have to pay, but you're not signing your life away either, there are no terms and conditions, just the same obligations you'd have as a citizen walking down the street.[6]

I love every bit of this, especially the 'building a playground' line, for that is exactly how I regard parkrun. Mr Sinton-Hewitt has provided a structure within which those who want to run together can do so. They can make it a race, a run or a stroll as they see fit. In designing it in such a multipurpose way, he's done a great thing for society. Just as we need our public buildings, our hospitals, schools and town halls, so too we need our playgrounds – and not just for children.

Thus I take the train to London to take part in the anniversary run. I feel anxious, as if this one really matters. I have travelled 185 miles to do it – even further than I did in France. I know I am reasonably fit; I am not suffering from any stress fractures or other pains. This should be my quickest 5K of the year. Trusting that I don't fall over or have some other accident, I should beat 20:30.

I wake at 3.55 a.m. I try to go back to sleep but lie awake, my mind shifting from subject to subject as if flicking through the pages of a book. After a while I look at my watch again: 5.38. I think about running, almost fantasising about the times I want to achieve. First mile in 6:25; second one in 6:35; third in 6:45 and then 40 seconds for the last 173 metres – that should get me home in 20:25. Then I go over the run again, and again, each imaginary run being faster than the last. Half an hour later the cars are passing outside. Half an hour after that, it is getting light. No point in trying to sleep any more.

As I walk through Bushy Park, I hear birdsong and see squirrels, a rabbit and many deer. This park must be a great asset to those who live nearby. When I have lived in cities it's always been the lack of nature that has got me down – the lack of a natural 'playground'. Here the deer are so tame they cross paths with the runners making their way to the start. I am sure someone must have a picture of a deer dressed in an apricot-coloured parkrun running vest, with 'Bushy Park' inscribed on its chest. Their tameness is a real contrast to the wildness of the flinchingly shy deer that live in the wooded hills above Moreton, or the one I saw on the parkrun in Ludlow.

By 8.45 there are well over a thousand people here, and more still making their way beneath the trees. A man speaks to us with a loudhailer and hands out prizes for the youngster who has attended the most parkruns, the most improved runner, the person who best embodies the spirit of parkrun, the champion parkrunning family (a family of four, who have done over a thousand runs between them) and the volunteer of the year. The speaker then talks about the first run here, and points to the spot where it started, about a hundred metres away. He calls out several names: three men and a woman step forward. These are four of the fabled 13 who took part in that first run. They are all smiling and looking pretty fit. The run director then organises a photograph of everyone who is wearing an apricot running vest. Unfortunately for me, after the photograph those in apricot are directed to join everyone else behind the 30-yard-wide starting line and, as there is insufficient space for them to pass behind us, they mingle with those at the front, forcing the rest of us backwards. I count nine rows of heads in front of me; this is not going to be a fast start.

The whistle goes and I jog over the grass, elbowed by one woman in apricot and almost tripped up by a child nearby. There are five or six hundred people in front of me. When I reach the path, dozens of runners are clogging it up. If I join them, I will be even slower. So I run across the grassy bumps alongside the path, trying to find a way on to the hard surface. Everyone around me seems very slow. 'Sorry,' I say, time and time again, as I squeeze between them. It is still chaotically crowded after two-thirds of a mile. At that point two big guys are running side by side, blocking the path. There is a space of about a foot between them. I call out 'excuse me' again and go for the gap. It isn't wide enough and one of them hits my arm with his.

'Oi! You're not supposed to barge through,' he shouts.

'I'm sorry,' I reply, turning back to face him, 'I beg your pardon.' He looks like someone who, if an apology was a small furry animal, would break its legs off, stuff it in his mouth and start chewing. So I just run faster. But the congestion has taken a toll. My watch tells me that my first mile is up: 6:41.

We make a sharp left turn by the edge of the park and I see people lined up ahead of me and chase them down, one by one. The second mile has taken me 6:36.

Better, I tell myself, and pursue the next person ahead. I catch him as we turn left and run alongside the lime trees by the road. I overtake more runners. We turn left again, onto a firm path. I set my sights on a woman in a green club vest about 80 metres ahead and try to catch up with her. We make a sharp right turn and quickly I close the gap and go past. Next is a man who looks to be in his fifties; I overtake him just in front of the rise before the bank of a pond. My watch beeps to tell me my third mile was also 6:36. As we rush towards the finish I overtake a final group. My time is 20:46. I've come 134th.

At the end of the day I look back on the run with a degree of satisfaction. It was the second-largest field there has ever been at a UK parkrun: 1,465 runners. My slow start cost me in the region of 20 seconds: all that weaving around trying to find a clear line took extra distance. But the real satisfaction isn't the performance, it's the pilgrimage. For when I check the details, there weren't just four of the original 13 parkrunners from 2004 here today; there were six. One of the volunteers at that first run was also running. What a phenomenon they have witnessed, from 13 runners to a huge, jostling crowd of 1,465 – plus another 2,530,097 people signed up to parkrun worldwide (at the time of writing). It is by far the world's biggest association of runners. And it only exists because one man had a good idea and the determination to make it happen.

Paul Sinton-Hewitt is one of those people who exemplifies the fact that individuals can make a difference. When I was at university reading for my first degree in the late 1980s I was repeatedly told that, historically, individuals don't matter. They are the mere crests of waves that briefly touch the sunlight and then disappear into the unfathomable depths. Only the deeper tides of history are important. As the years go by, however, I find myself disagreeing with that judgement more and more. Often a single person can make a decision that affects millions of people. What would the world be like today if Tim Berners-Lee had never developed the World Wide Web? Or Alexander Fleming had never discovered penicillin and Frank Colton had not developed the oral contraceptive pill? Parkrun might not have changed our lives as much as these things but it reminds us that individuals *can* make a difference. It is an important lesson for us and for our children. For therein lies a vestige of hope for our society.

32 | PASSION

14 October

Andy Gardner is joining me again, and Alexander too. We drop Oliver off at a chess tournament and head to the parkrun at Torbay Velodrome, where 276 runners are gathering. The weather forecasters have been talking about a heatwave but it is showing no sign of appearing on the South Devon coast. The sky is swirling with grey clouds. I wonder about the wetness of the grass but have no time to check it before we are lining up for the run. We wish each other good luck and then suddenly the countdown is underway and we are off.

A man in his early fifties heads straight to the front, with a younger fellow hot on his heels. They are well away within a matter of seconds. Eight or nine others follow them, and then Alexander. I am right on his shoulder, testing my strength against his. He knows I am there, and every time I advance on him he speeds up. But his inability to keep going at the faster speed shows me he is not going to be a match for me today. Sure enough, after half a mile, I run past him. Immediately I focus on the next runner and work away at reducing the gap. One or two others catch up with me and go past but that doesn't matter. I know I am making progress. My watch beeps: 6:11 for the first mile. I pursue two runners in club vests and catch them at the next arm of the velodrome circuit. A woman in her early thirties appears alongside me and overtakes. I recognise her: until recently she was the female record-holder at one of the local runs, so I know I'm doing well, even if this is one of her slower days. Two hundred metres further on I become aware of a runner right behind me. I glance back: he is in his thirties, tall and athletic-looking. I recognise him from running alongside him here in Torbay, earlier in the year. His name is Gary Burman. *He won't be behind me for long*, I tell myself. But I am wrong. Gary is using me as a pacer. My watch beeps again: 6:28 for the second mile. Twenty minutes is within sight.

Except it isn't.

No sooner have we run into the field than I realise this third mile is going to be very slow. The grass is as long as I've ever seen it and wet too. There are muddy patches. My target now has to shift to something more like 20:30. But it is harder on the grass. Gary shoots past me. So too does one of the club runners I passed earlier. The only consolation is that the woman who passed me is slowing up and possibly within reach. As we circumnavigate the field, the gap between us closes. I turn the last corner and go for it. She also finds a last bit of speed to overtake the man in front and I finish 5 seconds behind her, in thirteenth. My time is 20:36. I can't believe I slowed up so much. That third mile in the field was 7:10. It may be my fastest parkrun of the year so far – by one second – but I cannot shake off the disappointment not to have run close to 20 minutes.

At the end of the afternoon, when I drive back to Torbay to pick up Oliver, my thoughts on the run are strangely varied. One great thing is that I have rediscovered the thrill of finding out how fast I can run, something that excites all runners in their first few timed events. My age grade was 71.6 per cent, my highest so far this year. I am also pleased with the fact that I was in the fastest 5 per cent of the field. I suppose I should be pleased, full stop. But I cannot be happy. I failed to reach my main target, and no amount of statistical juggling can make up for that.

It is Oliver who brings me back to reality, when he comes out of his chess match.

'How was it?' I ask him.

'It was good. Although not brilliant.'

'How many games did you win?'

'None of them. Four of my five opponents had a TPG (Tournament Performance Grade) of over a hundred. One was a hundred and sixty-nine, which is the highest I've yet seen. As for the last game, I played too quickly and threw it away. But I'm really glad I turned up.'

I feel humbled by my son, whose generosity of spirit can make even losing five straight games into something positive. I feel humbled too by Andy, who had the grace to run again after our gentlemen's triathlon. I feel as if I am greedy – that I am not satisfied even with one of my best performances. Greedy, greedy, greedy...

But no, it is not greed. It's love. The very object of my desire – 20 minutes – is like a stunningly beautiful woman. I cannot take my eyes off her. She stands in the middle of a line of statuesque Muses. At the far end are her sisters, the utterly unattainable 15 and 16 minutes, whose supermodel wonderfulness is out of this world. Next to them I see the elegant figures of 17 and 18 minutes, like sirens who would lure me to my death. Their sophisticated sibling, 19 minutes, watches me stare at them with an air of wry amusement. But for me, 20 minutes is special. She teases me. She's already let me kiss her once, last year, and I am besotted. As for her other sisters, 21 and 22 minutes, they are too busy with the attentions of other people and, anyway, I am not mesmerised by them. Here's the truth. I am not in love with the idea of running 20:36 but with running 19:59 or faster. That's why anything less leaves me unsatisfied.

———————

Now my mind turns to the Great West Run: the fourth of the five half marathons I resolved to run this year. After my stress fracture and doing the Torbay half marathon at the end of June without any training, I forbade myself from running more than 5 miles for 2 months, to allow my femurs to strengthen. Only in September did I dare do an 8-mile run. I've only done two more 8-mile and two 11-mile runs since then. And all of them were slow. I am thus not in the sort of shape necessary to run 13 miles up and down the hilly roads around Exeter in a decent time.

My Saturday evening is spent going out for a pizza with a friend and then going on to a party. Not the ideal preparation for a half marathon, you might say. But there are reasons. My friend's fiancée is on her hen night (with Sophie, amongst others), and the party is being held to celebrate the birthday of another good friend. I restrict myself to two glasses of wine and leave at 11 p.m. Jonathan Camp stops me at the door.

'This has got to be the first time I've ever seen you leave a party before midnight,' he declares.

'It's love,' I tell him. 'A goddess. You may think that Marilyn Monroe's 36–24–34 are the dimensions of desire. But a 100-minute half marathon is even more alluring.'

100 minutes? Who am I kidding?

15 October

Despite my early night, I sleep badly, waking to see every grinning demon hour of the clock: 2.15; 3.36; 4.04; 5.57. Eventually I get up at 6.15 and ready myself for the day. Coffee. Chocolate. It is still dark outside.

I check my email. There is a message from a friend, which says: 'I think it's the Great West Run today. Best of luck. I hope you get the time you want but most of all enjoy the event.'

Enjoy the event.

Suddenly I see sense in following that advice. *Give up on that 100-minute target, Ian. Just do this as a slow run.*

Don't bother with your watch. Just enjoy moving through the air, like you do on an easy training run.

I drive into Exeter and arrive early at the runners' park, adjacent to the arena. I soon bump into a fellow Moretonian. It turns out that our little town is to be represented by half a dozen runners, including regular parkrunners Bob Small and Anne-Marie Baker (she of the lovely smile). I watch everyone prepare, taking their places in the starting pens. I opt for the slower one, with an expected finish time of between 1:45:00 and 2 hours. With that one little gesture, I take all the pressure off myself, and begin to look forward to the race.

I start gently, just jogging. I resolve not to look at my watch. I can honestly say that it is delightful, making my way through the crowd of runners, with people cheering us on both sides of the street. Even the daunting first hill is not a worry. Thousands of people are out in support in the city centre. I hear my watch beep the completion of the second mile and ignore it. There are hundreds of competitors ahead and I don't care. Down New North Road we run, and I stay on the left, as if out for a run by myself. Then we head out to Stoke Woods. I am moving along happily beneath the trees when I see the 5-mile sign. About a minute later the leader comes back the other way behind a car with a digital readout on its roof: we are 39:04 into the race. *Damn! I was trying to forget about times. But that means I must be doing about 7:40 per mile.*

What did I say about times and running in chapter five? That we need times to make sense of our performances.

Well, that's not always true. Right now, time is a distraction. It's about as inappropriate as trying to measure hope.

Around the 7-mile mark a chap about my age in an orange running shirt starts chatting about what time I am aiming for. He tells me his best to date is 1:43 but he's aiming for 1:40. He is very pleasant but right now I don't really want to talk. I am thinking ahead to the big hill that will be practically the whole tenth mile. I am beginning to feel a little tired. I take it easy on the lower slope and then take it even easier on the steep section. Many people are out in support of their families here – giving them encouragement just where they need it most. At the end, I see the 10-mile sign with some relief. Only a parkrun to go now. But it's tough, and my lack of long-distance running is not just showing, it's hurting.

A man bearing a green flag stating '1:45' appears on my right and runs past me.

You can't avoid times on a race. Everyone is so keen on them that *not knowing* is not an option. But *not caring* is. I run around the corner at the bottom of Old Tiverton Road and start the long climb up Pinhoe Road, watching the pacer move ever further away. I feel I'm really not cut out to do half marathons. The 5K times that I want to run stand like a row of Greek goddesses but the nymphs of the half marathon just don't hold that much attraction for me. I find 1:45:00 a fairly plain girl, to tell the truth, and my only reason for fancying her now is my worry that otherwise I'll be paired up with one of her less-desirable sisters. One with warts, varicose veins, bad breath and a wooden leg.

Then a second 1:45 pacer goes past.

Oh, for heaven's sake, isn't one enough?

As I run, I watch their little green flags move further and further ahead. *Does that 1:45 time mean nothing to you, Ian?* Yesterday I asked myself whether I was greedy not to be satisfied with my parkrun. Today I have to ask myself, am I so spoilt that I can't be bothered to improve my time? After all, I cannot pretend anymore that I am only running for enjoyment. This is really painful. The pacers are well ahead now, probably 150 and 100 metres respectively. It's now or never.

Are you going to catch them, Ian?

We are coming up to the 12-mile mark.

Yes, you are.

I lengthen my stride and quicken my pace, and try to close the gap. The crowds around us are growing as we near the arena. There are several runners between me and the pacers. But I disregard everyone else except the two men with flags. They too have decided to pick up their speed. *Okay, Ian, you are going to close within 50 metres of them at the turning to Summer Lane. Then you'll have 400 metres to catch them on that hill, and another 400 in the arena to build a good distance between you and them. Go!*

Although I am now feeling very tired, I close up on the second pacer. Turning into Summer Lane I have both of them in my sights. But running up the hill to the arena they start to get away from me again. *Damn!* My body tries to tell me that it isn't far to go now, and it doesn't matter if I don't catch them, I can stop soon. But I try not to listen. Spectators are clapping and cheering. I concentrate on the men with the flags. I force myself fast up the approach to the arena but they are still well ahead. Now I'm in the arena, pounding over its springy brick-red surface. There is a woman in a yellow South West Road Runners shirt 5 metres ahead of me, and three men in a bunch about 15 metres ahead of her, and the two pacers about another 10 metres ahead of them. I follow the woman for half the lap, keeping steady, and then, with 200 metres to go, I sprint like I've never sprinted before in my life. I fly past her on the bend, catch up with the men, swerve to the right as one steps out in front of me, and then charge as fast as I possibly can towards the pacers. I catch and overtake them with 2 or 3 metres to spare. My pace crossing the finish line is 4:59 per mile. Someone pushes an already-finished runner out of the way and lets me charge through. My time is 1:44:47.

At the moment of finishing, as I stumble forward, I am suddenly dizzy. I sway from side to side just like in Bath, and head to a patch of grass on which to lie down. When I get up again, I am still not right. I am light-headed. For the next 10 minutes I pass through the crowds seeing great gladness in people's expressions and, in some cases, lonely despondency. I feel like a ghost walking among a mass of strangers living 20 years after I am dead. This is what it will be like: such familiar humanity and such unfamiliar faces.

Then Bob Small hails me and I go over to him and embrace him. Although only 6 weeks short of his seventieth birthday, he has run the distance in 1:57:36. Twenty years older than me and yet only 12 minutes slower. I want to be like him when I grow up.

What does it all amount to at the end of the day?

A lesson in passion.

You can't pretend to love things you don't love. Don't get me wrong – I do love being able to run for 13 miles – but my affection for long distances diminishes with the weight placed upon their times. My love for shorter runs, however, increases as the times become more significant and exciting. The message is clear. You are going to do best at the challenge that attracts you most strongly, which will not allow you to be satisfied with underachievement. It is through pursuing our true passions that we most confidently address the rest of the world – and thereby gain the greatest satisfaction.

33 THE LANDSCAPE OF THINKING

28 October

Everything was looking so good after the Great West Run. I recovered quickly and was out jogging 2 days later. However, later that week, during one of the concerts I had arranged as part of my New Year's resolutions, I started to feel a pain in my left knee. It grew rapidly. By the interval, I was in agony. No need for a doctor's diagnosis: this was gout, from which I have suffered for the last 11 or 12 years. The pain worsened considerably in the second half of the concert, as I knew it would. I was unable to sit still; it was all I could do to stop crying out. Yet I could not leave the building. As the person in charge, it was my duty at the end to thank the performer, and then help the sound engineer and other assistants dismantle the stage and clear up all the technical paraphernalia. So there I was, sitting in the front row, writhing and wincing. Afterwards, all I could do was give directions to others. By midnight I was in bed, shouting out with the pain, my teeth chattering as if I had a fever, sweating and just wanting the intense anguish to end.

I asked Sophie to bring me whisky. She located a bottle of Glenfiddich and I downed half of it, to knock me out.

Gout, in case you don't know, is an ailment whereby high levels of uric acid cause needle-like crystals to form inside the joints. This is far more painful than sticking needles into your knee from the outside. At its worst, any movement, no matter how slight, is excruciating. It can happen in any joint: I've had it in a big toe, both knees and once in a wrist. The knees are the worst. After my fourth or fifth bad attack, 10 years ago, I started taking allopurinol every day to control the creation of uric acid. But despite the medication, I was in agony after the concert. The only time I have seen anyone in as much pain is when Sophie was giving birth. Not that you can compare gout and childbirth – there are more or less painful forms of both – but I imagine that many people will agree that a bad gout attack is up there with the most intense pain an otherwise healthy man is likely ever to feel, just as childbirth ticks that box for most women.

Fortunately, this was not the worst attack I have ever had. Nevertheless, even a minor one does a lot of damage and makes it very painful to move the leg in the days immediately afterwards. Running was out of the question. I could hardly walk. I had particular difficulty climbing the stairs, having to haul my left leg up each one individually, keeping my knee as straight as possible. Thus I spent my days in inactivity again. At night, I felt the spasms in my unexercised muscles as they spontaneously contracted tighter and tighter, until after 2 or 3 seconds they turned into intense balls of pain. In the daytime,

I felt my fitness dripping away, like wax melting beneath the heat of a candle. It seemed my whole body was weeping. Sophie told me I shouldn't even think about leaving the house. But I could not go on like this. After a few days, I decided to take matters into my own hands. I waited until Sophie had gone to work, and then went for a walk. The following day, feeling much better, I again waited until she was out, and went for a gentle 5-mile run. It was blissful. Probably the most enjoyable run I have ever done. It was like pouring away all my troubles down the sink, and seeing them spiralling round and round as they went down the plug. A neighbour quietly told my wife I'd been running but I simply smiled as Sophie gave me the benefit of her views on the matter.

Thus it is that today I am not sitting in an armchair with my leg up but driving into Exeter to do the parkrun there with both my sons, my brother Robbie and Andy Gardner. It is a glorious morning, the sun rejoicing in the green and golden leaves of autumn. As we drive down Dunsford Hill, the view of the cathedral looks particularly fine: its two towers proudly standing like giant chess pieces above the roofs of the city as they have done since they were built in the early twelfth century. We've been chatting all the way. It turns out we are all suffering from a slight fuzzy-headedness. It was Robbie's youngest son's birthday yesterday and we celebrated as a family. In my joyous state I promised Alexander £50 if he beats me in a parkrun by the end of the year. 'Make it five-hundred pounds and I'll make sure it happens,' he replied. 'I'll train every day.'

I start off telling myself – as I so often do – that there is no need to try to run fast today. I contrast this wishy-washiness with my determination to run so soon after the gout. The test of determination is whether it resists pressure, or so it seems to me. And to do that it has to be flawless from the outset. Any crack in it and, like a faulty water jug, it won't do the job at all.

At the 1-mile mark I glance back between the trees to see Alexander about 30 metres behind me.

In the field the ground is soft and wet. The marker flags have been placed well inside the perimeter again. At 20-minute pace, cutting the corners by that much reduces your time by at least 7 seconds. Therefore I keep to the very edge, in order to make up the full 5K. Alexander notices me running a longer route and immediately sees his opportunity, putting on a spurt of speed. *Not today, young man.* I run harder. That element of my determination – not to let my son beat me – is not cracked. Those things you most want to achieve don't require any extra drive or self-discipline. You just do them because nothing is stopping you.

At a literary festival not long ago, I spoke to half a dozen other writers about running. They all told me sagely that running is bad for you. It does too much damage to the body, they said. Likewise they all agreed that nothing is as good for a writer as walking. This amused me as clearly none of them ran and none of them had sold as many books as I had. 'You get so many good ideas when walking,' insisted one elderly literary gentleman.

'True,' I replied. 'Some of my best ideas have occurred to me on walks. But that doesn't mean you don't get them when running too.'

'Such as?' a woman asked.

'I think about everything from equality to how selfish some people can be, and the essence of a good marriage, and how fussy I can be, and how proud I am of my sons when they run. I think about distances and times a great deal. I do a lot of maths in my head, working out paces and how far I have yet to go, that sort of thing.'

'It sounds very boring if you ask me,' the elderly gentleman said.

'But you don't understand,' I replied. 'I don't run to have beautiful thoughts. I run to stay fit, to feel ready for anything, and to focus on what it means to be alive. You think differently when running. You think under pressure. The urgency of your movements acts like a knife, slicing your thought processes up into small segments. It is true that you can't sustain any great progression of ideas – at least, not like you can when walking. You think in short sentences, not paragraphs. But that too can be great for the imagination. The only drawback is that you have to put so much mental energy into making your body work hard that you are lucky if even a few good ideas stick.'

As I run out of the field back onto the tarmac path, with Alexander dropping further behind me, I wonder what ideas will 'stick' from this run. Is that idea about the test of determination resisting pressure worth preserving?

I don't know. Just as I said, running chops up your ideas into small pieces, so that you can't really gauge the quality of your thoughts while you are still going. But the test of determination is worth remembering to mull over later. I can see it has potential. Perhaps it could be developed. Is true determination a matter of resisting all other temptations? No, *self-discipline* is the ability to resist temptations. Determination is being so focused on a particular outcome that one does not even see there are any other temptations.

What I know will 'stick' is that the very act of thinking takes place in a sort of inner landscape. The mental environment you find yourself in when running is a very different sort of terrain from the mental space you are in when walking, and that in turn is very different from your mental space when sitting still. When you are running, you think as if you are in a jungle. You can't see very far but ideas spring out at you rapidly as you go past trees and creepers, bushes and boulders, constantly aware of threats and dangers. Here's one, there's another, and here is a third, and soon you have forgotten the first one because you're too busy dealing with the fourth. When walking, the landscape of the mind is more like the countryside. It is calmer than the jungle. You can see much further but there are still enough features to inspire you and set your mind going in a new direction. And when you are sitting still, your mind is far out on a calm sea, aware only of the gentle waves and the blue sky. Your ideas come from within, and only from within: there are no obstacles. You can see in every direction as far as the curvature of the Earth will allow.

The landscapes of thinking: I am not sure that any one of them is better than the other two. In fact, I think the festival writers were wrong to say that walking is better. It seems to me that the optimum way to think is to benefit from them all.

34 | FAMILY AND FAMILIARITY

4 November

This weekend Sophie and I are visiting my cousins, Charles and Sarah Read, who live in Bickley, a suburban district of south London. This is not far from Petts Wood, where I grew up. Charles is a cousin on my father's side and Sarah a cousin on my mother's. Thus their daughters Hannah and Gemma are as closely related to me as their parents. Both girls have been persuaded to do Beckenham Place parkrun with me. I can't blame them for being reluctant: it is raining when we set off and still raining when we reach Beckenham Place.

As we wait beneath umbrellas, I tell Charles that he and I are the very distant relatives of a world record holder. On 15 November 1858, a young man called St Vincent Hammick ran the mile in 4:45, which was then the world record for an amateur (the professional record was 4:23). St Vincent was our sixth cousin three-times-removed, our mutual ancestors being Henry and Dorcas Hammick, who were married in 1645. I add that, with a connection as distant as that, probably everyone else here today at Beckenham Park is more closely related to a world record holder than we are. 'Some of them are probably more closely related to the same guy,' comments Sarah. This is almost certainly true. We're all more intimately related than we think. As mentioned in chapter 18, King Edward II and his nemesis Sir Roger Mortimer both had so many descendants by 1500 that it is extremely unlikely anyone of predominantly English descent is not descended from one of them. That means everyone is at least a twenty-second cousin of everyone else, give or take a few removals.

When the run director starts us off, I see a number of men charge ahead across the path. They are keen here in Beckenham! Definitely more closely related to St Vincent Hammick than I am. At the first bend I count 24 people in front of me. Running feels hard – not just because of the wet grass but also because I don't know the route. Unfamiliar journeys always seem to take much longer than those you know. But I follow the line of runners and settle into a rhythm. At the end of the first lap, Charles, Sarah and Sophie shout encouragement from beneath their umbrellas. 'You're twenty-seventh,' Sophie calls out as I begin the second lap. Two people overtake me, and I overtake one. Another one up, another one down. It stays like that until the end of the run.

Looking out of the car window on the way home I turn over this point about unfamiliarity, how much further everything seems when you see it for the first time. I toy with the idea of running around places I am familiar with – all the nearby streets and parks I used to know in my childhood – some of which I have not seen for 30 or 40 years. It is an attractive idea. In fact, would it not be interesting to run around everywhere that takes in my early life? I resolve to do just that in the morning.

———————

5 November

I hear the grandfather clock in the hallway chime 5 o'clock. Then 6 o'clock. When it rings seven times I get up and pull on my running clothes. I creep from the room, so as not to wake Sophie, and step outside into the bright Bromley morning.

I have no idea how far I will run, nor which way I will go. I just start running. First I jog past the house where my aunt has lived since before I was born, then past the place where my grandmother lived when I was a child, then along to Bickley Park School. I turn left and head down to the junior school, which was called Bickley Parva in my day, where I was taught from the age of four until seven. In just the first 2 miles, a hundred memories have entered my mind – from being given crisps by my grandmother from her walk-in larder, to the headmaster making sure that the windows of the dormitory at Bickley Park were open at night (a large room that had no carpets or curtains, I might add) with the result that one day I woke to find snow on the end of my bed. It was there that I won an 800-metre athletics heat at the age of eleven, in a time of 3:13 (an age grading of just 63 per cent, it turns out). I recall being taken by my parents to see Bickley Parva for the first time, and watching the 'big boys' – who were then aged five – enter an assembly hall to collect their morning milk: they drank it sitting on benches ranged around the hall. I remember the wood-panelled dining room, as silent as only an empty wood-panelled room can be, with all our personal napkin rings placed carefully on the long wooden tables, and the dust in the sunlight settling on them. I am reminded too of being told to bend over one day – to feel the thwack of the headmaster's shoe on my backside.

That was another age.

On I run, up to Bromley Common. Charles and I were once taken to see Chipperfield's Circus here in the late seventies – complete with elephants, monkeys, lions and other exotic animals. That too was another age. Then along up to Bromley high street, which I have not seen for 20 years. I pass the department store where I worked one holiday as an eighteen-year-old in a carpet department, where a prank-playing colleague once slipped a centrefold from a pornographic magazine into my order book to embarrass me in front of a customer. At the top of the high street I pass the church and run down across the park where I injured myself in a bicycle accident at the age of seventeen. I had been sent home in disgrace from my boarding school; that night I got drunk with some friends and crashed my bike going down the steep path, landing on my head. I almost gave my parents a heart attack as I tried to creep into their bedroom in the early hours, losing consciousness as I did so, crashing into my mother's dressing table and leaving a great quarter-circle of bright blood smeared on the wallpaper as I fell.

The morning, the sun, the familiarity – this is bliss! I run on to Shortlands and up to the flat in Scotts Lane where the family lived in the early eighties. There is my bedroom window, not looking out for me at all, like the eyes of a skull, staring at infinity. More memories flit before my eyes – from listening to The Doors' *Soft Parade* every morning before heading off to work in the Christmas decorations department at Harrods in 1985, to drinking too much rum and blackcurrant on New Year's Eve that year, and being sick out of my bedroom window (I wince with embarrassment when recalling the downstairs' neighbour's reaction on New Year's Day).

I run back from Shortlands to Bromley and the park I mentioned before, where now I recall doing a 10-mile sponsored walk in my school shoes at the age of ten. It was for Help the Aged. I developed the most appalling blisters; I never once thought about being old myself. I run past the tennis courts and up to the Churchill Theatre and library, which were partly designed by my father. When I was eight, my mother would lift me up so I could see through the apertures in the hoarding to look at the foundations being built. Years later I would spend hours in the reference library in that same building, discovering historical wonders such as *The Dictionary of National Biography* and *The Complete Peerage* – tools of my trade these days. Then I come to the market square: it is pedestrianised now but back in 1979 it was normally filled with slow-moving traffic. I used to look out of the car window at the cover of Blondie's *Parallel Lines* in the front of a record shop there. It took me months to save up enough pocket money to buy a copy.

I run back along Widmore Road to Bickley and on to Petts Wood, and all the way through to Petts Wood Road, where I lived for the first 15 years of my life. An Indian food shop I pass along the way was then one of Petts Wood's two toyshops. The proprietor used to give me free paint whenever I bought a new set of toy soldiers. I turn to see the premises that was once my local bookshop, where I bought my Asterix books. And on the other side of the road, that is where the butcher's shop was, where I was regularly sent to buy horsemeat for our dog. This is where my friend Amos and I had fights with our scarves and ties on the way home from school, or practised long-distance spitting, or had snowball fights. Here is the stream where I fished for sticklebacks; there is the tree where my mother used to rest on the way back up the hill with the shopping; there is the house where Anna, my first sweetheart, lived; and there are the two round windows of my childhood bedroom, from which I used to wave to Anna in the mornings, and where I spent so many hours thinking, reading and listening to music – and dreaming of her.

This is such an unbelievably rich experience that I just continue to run and run. The very fact I am connecting these places on foot seems to shrink the whole of my childhood to a small patch of ground. I run down Poverest Road, past the ancient burial place of Saxon warriors whose relics now lie in the local museum. I run through the Priory Gardens where my mother would take me to feed the ducks when I was three or four, and then up Orpington high street, where I recall buying Beethoven's *Ninth Symphony* at the age of ten and 'Down in the Tube Station at Midnight' by The Jam at eleven. All this familiarity just makes every step a joy. I pass the branch of the National Westminster Bank where I first recall my father using a cashpoint machine: in those days you were sent punch-cards in the post, which you put in the machine in return for £10 notes. I run past the electricity appliance shop where my mother worked in 1977, and where all the family met up one evening before going to watch *Star Wars* at the cinema on the other side of the road. And here is the street where I was almost killed at the age of nine, when I was left alone for the day and took the dog for a long walk: I heard a siren and a screech of brakes and turned to see a car pursued by a police van coming straight towards me at high speed with its wheels on the narrow footpath. It veered off at the last moment – but in my mind it didn't. It is still there, coming straight towards me.

The fragmented mental landscape of running is the perfect way to revisit these places. The ten thousand bite-sized moments of realisation and memory are a stream of delight. It is like seeing my life flash before my eyes – only not because I'm on the point of death. In fact, I feel more alive than ever, running up the hill beside Orpington Station and on to Crofton, and then through Petts Wood again, along the shopping parade. This is the place where my family first encountered Chinese food, in the form of the Sun-Do takeaway, in the late 1970s. And look! Sun-Do is still there. The greengrocer's shop has gone, and so has the travel agent, the toyshop, the Woolworths and the camera shop – all these premises now accommodate other businesses – but the Chinese takeaway has become part of my heritage.

When I finally come to a halt, back at Charles and Sarah's house, I look at my watch. I have covered 19.42 miles in 2 hours 44 minutes and 52 seconds. That's further than I've ever run before. And the pace is much faster than I would have run had I been intending to cover almost 20 miles. I've lulled myself into running further and faster than my limitations. Due to the pure familiarity of it.

How many meanings unfold from just this one run! There's the obvious point about my relaxed and happy state of mind, and how running down memory lane after such a long time is exhilarating. This was a rare instance of a run that was both hugely enjoyable and deeply satisfying. But what really captivates me is the awareness that we can recover so many memories. Very few remain at our fingertips; most lie buried. But we can uncover thousands of them with just one run, as if the very act of jogging disturbs the topsoil of the mind. I was literally 'jogging my memory'. Would all those recollections have come back if I had just been *walking* down memory lane? Perhaps. But I could not have covered almost 20 miles in less than 3 hours had I not run, and so I could not have experienced such an intense concentration of memories.

I am left with an overwhelming impression of just how many things happen in the course of a childhood. When I was young, I was still learning and everything was unfamiliar, so my early years seemed at the time to be an unknown route – one that took forever to complete. Now each year disappears with far greater rapidity. But today I rediscovered something of the richness of childhood, and how much goes into the making of a character. And the amazing thing is that so much of it is so ordinary and yet fascinating – for it is the very experience which has shaped us. Later, when I tell my wife and cousins where I have been, I think back to the occasions when Charles and Sarah would have met as children at our house in Petts Wood Road, and no one would have thought that they would one day marry and have daughters, nor that those girls would run together with me in Beckenham, nor that I would run all around the area at the age of fifty, remembering and reminding myself what it was to be a boy, when my dreams were a mixture of music, girls and medieval archaeology, and before that, when my mother would lift me up to look through the hoarding of the past at my father's great, unbuilt theatre of the future.

This has been the run of my life – in more ways than one. Everyone has their own version, an equivalent place. Go and run there, I urge you. It will be special.

35 | DECISION-MAKING

11 November

Today is Armistice Day. I regard the commemoration with mixed feelings. On the one hand I have great respect for those who, when duty called, signed up to fight for their country. On the other, I find a lot of the solemn reflection so arbitrary and illogical that I feel obliged to question it. From an early age I thought, why do we only remember the wars of the twentieth century? What about those who gave their lives in the French Revolutionary Wars, the Crimean War and the Boer War? What about the Hundred Years' War, the Wars of the Roses and the Civil Wars? They weren't much fun either. Then at a more mature age I started to wonder why we only commemorate those who died? Surely the courageous thing was to agree to fight in the first place, whether as a volunteer or professional soldier. My views changed direction again when I became a historian and learned that 11 November is also Martinmas: the day when people traditionally slaughtered all the animals that they were not planning to feed through the winter. It seemed strange to choose a day set aside for the mass killing of animals to commemorate the mass killing of men. It seemed even stranger when I came across the Animals in War Memorial in Park Lane, London, which records the killing of millions of horses and hundreds of thousands of dogs and pigeons in the two World Wars. Looking at the poppy wreaths on that memorial, there seemed to be a disjuncture in the morality. None of those animals chose to meet the fate that awaited them, but nor did any of those slaughtered for food. Therefore, as we don't build expensive monuments in Park Lane to the bacon and eggs we have for breakfast, why do we do so for the horses, pigeons and dogs that we send off to be slaughtered in other ways? Call me cynical, but I can't help feeling that that memorial says more about the politics of human conscience than it does about animals. And once you think that, you wonder about the whole act of remembering as a society. Is not all commemoration a tacit expression of our guilt that we make our young people go off and kill other people?

Nevertheless, I do wear a poppy each year. I do so for several reasons. First I remember my great-grandfather, who was a gunner in France in the First World War, who was profoundly shocked by his experiences there. Next I think of the horrendous bombing of towns and cities – both in the Blitz in this country and in the firestorms we caused in Dresden and Hamburg, and in the calamity we caused more recently in Iraq. I think of the terrible loss that parents must have felt, when one day the postman did not deliver a letter home from their son but a brief telegram from his commanding officer. I think of the tragedies experienced by many of those who survived: some shell-shocked, some who never heard their friends laugh again and yet could not forget their laughter, and some who felt guilty for simply being the sole member of their squadron to survive. I think particularly of Sophie's grandfather, Ted Baker, who was an army chaplain in the Second World War. He died 20 years ago but I know his story well. His duty was that of comforting men in the face of death. As he was waiting to get off the troopship during the D-Day landings, an eighteen-year-old lad standing beside him shot himself in the foot on purpose, hoping to be invalided back to England. Instead, the young man was told that staying on the ship was not an option. Ted helped him off the boat and into the water, and then dragged him over his shoulder and pulled him up the beach under machine-gun fire, until they reached safety. Then he had to hold countless burial services for those who had not made it – which proved as emotional and traumatic as the actual landing. After the war he wrote a memoir of his experiences, which includes many instances of having to console frightened men and, later, having to write to their mothers and widows, telling them how their sons and husbands had died and what their final messages were. He never properly recovered from the trauma.

There is no cenotaph at which to remember people like him, or to mark the true devotion he showed his fellow men. He survived: his name is on no memorial. But his service to king and country was as great as any man's. He put humanity first. I wear a poppy for him most of all.

The weather is grim. Oliver, Andy and I walk across the garden, avoiding the slippery wet flagstones of the path. There are leaves everywhere, being blown around the wall by the garage. The copper beech is almost bare. If you could draw a picture of a windy sky – one that resembles a gale simply through its turbulent clouds and shades of grey – this is what it would look like. Nevertheless, we are in a sprightly mood as we drive off to Torquay. Andy says he is really looking forward to this run. Already he is setting himself targets: 26 minutes today. The rain, however, does not bode well. Moreover, it's not just today's rain that will encumber us, it's also the rain that has fallen over the past week. Sure enough, when we arrive, the path around the field looks like a quagmire.

But we are resolved. We are light-heartedly determined. And even if our times today do not turn out to be our fastest, they may well still be our best in terms of competitiveness, for everyone else will have to deal with the same mud. And a hard course will favour the brave and committed.

What do I want to achieve? When I last ran here I was in the fastest 5 per cent. Therefore I set myself the task of doing it again. About two hundred people are gathering for the start. That means I need to finish in the first ten.

That is going to be hard. If the weather is bad, it's normally only the dedicated runners who turn up. But then without much time for preparation, I hear, 'Three, two, one, go!' And we are away.

I start off in ninth but soon lose a couple of places as faster runners overtake. I settle into a routine, running at a little over 6-minute pace. After about half a mile, a devil on my shoulder tells me, *You could just take this one easy, Ian. After all, it won't be a fast time because of all the mud in the third mile.* But then an angel on the other shoulder reminds me, *You promised yourself that you'd try to finish in the top 5 per cent. Is your promise worth so very little that already you are prepared to break it?*

After completing the first mile in 6:12 I become aware of a man behind me, steadily following me. I wonder if it is Gary Burman using me as his pacer again; I saw him on the start line. I snatch a quick glance: sure enough, it is him. I smile, and wonder how long I can keep him behind me this time. We pound around the next couple of bends and around the hairpin and overtake someone who has fallen back from the leading group. Now he edges past. I try to keep close to him. As we leave the velodrome and head into the field, I am only a couple of seconds behind. But then there is the mud. No avoiding it. I am slipping all over the place. I aim for the longer grass, which is less slippery but no faster. Gary pulls away from me. I just can't run on this stuff and I let myself slow down. A young lad runs past me, his feet hardly sinking into the ground at all. Then a man about my age runs past. Then another, a taller man, in a black shirt. I follow the two of them, as the second one overtakes the first. Four hundred metres to go. Three hundred. I can't sprint on the grass as I will just sink into it but soon there will be gravel and then a solid surface. I increase my pace and catch the nearer man. I put on a little extra speed to make sure I get past him cleanly and pursue the runner in the black shirt. He senses me there and starts to sprint. I am almost alongside him. Now we are on the gravel. He is not giving in. Around the bend we go at breakneck pace. I can't run any faster. Neither of us is letting go. On and on – *keep going, Ian! KEEP GOING!* – all the way to the line. I win our little tussle by about 30 centimetres, to a round of applause from those watching. 'Well done, top-ten finish,' says the man handing out the tokens, giving me number ten. I've done it! I congratulate my adversary and shake hands with Gary Burman too, who has finished seventh. I then sit down on a stile to catch my breath.

My time is 21:10 – slower than my last run here, as expected. But did I achieve my target of being in the top 5 per cent? If there were two hundred people here, then yes. But maybe there weren't quite that many. I will have to wait until all the results are in to find out.

What I take away from this run is a thought about decision-making.

Think back to those men who went overseas to fight for king and country. They may have had little say in their going – especially those who were conscripted – but they all subsequently made many more choices, which ultimately led to victory. You can think of the war as one great tree of decisions, in which those taken by the political masters affected millions of people, and then those millions of people all made thousands of other decisions that affected millions more, as well as each other, and so on, cascading down from the political leadership. And yet what is a decision? On the one hand it is straightforward. On the other, you can approach a fork in a road and not know until the very last instant which way you will go. Indeed, you can still be in two minds as you find yourself walking one way without really knowing why. Today I was telling myself one minute that I was going to do my best to finish in the top 5 per cent and the next I was telling myself that I could relax. Somehow enough resolution remained for me to put in a sprint finish. But was that sprinting a decision-making process? Was it not just my character deciding for me? I can't answer that question fully. I can give you my gut reaction – yes, it was a decision, because I could have chosen at any instant to let him go ahead of me – but I don't believe it is actually that simple. Why did I not choose to put in the extra effort to stay ahead of Gary? I didn't feel I had a choice, believing him too strong for me. But how did I know? Sometimes a decision evolves in your mind without you having much control.

So what?

A few days ago I was standing in South Street, Exeter, looking in the window of a charity shop, wondering whether

I should buy the copy of *Eighteenth-Century Exeter* that I could see in the window. Suddenly a fight broke out right behind me, less than 2 metres away, between a hysterical young man, who was white, and an Asian man, also in his twenties, who was accompanied by two Asian friends. I have never tried to stop a fight before in my life, and I had no wish to involve myself now. But there was nowhere for me to go. I was trapped, right there. I could only watch and listen as the white chap shouted abuse and kept trying to punch his adversary. The following account of what happened next is from a note that I wrote immediately after the incident:

One of the Asian companions tried to hold the white guy at bay, but he was having none of it and kept coming at his victim. It looked like he had called the first Asian a name or said something derogatory about his race, as the Asian was shouting 'This is as much my home as yours'. The white guy was beyond reason, however, and was constantly trying to hit him. I just stood there, doing my best to stay out of it. But then, suddenly, the white guy broke through the cordon of the two companions and headbutted his victim hard in the face. There was an appalling crack and a second later they all started fighting, three against one. Punches were flung to faces and body, on both sides. It all looked pretty inept to me but it was as violent as they could manage – you don't need to be a professional to do serious damage to someone – and I reckoned it was about to get worse. So I felt I had to do something. I stepped in between them, and forcibly broke them apart. No one hit me. I stood with my arms outstretched, facing the white man. I told him that there would only be bad consequences, that he should leave these guys alone, that there were three of them. But he would not listen. He kept trying to get to his victim. I had to hold him back, with my palms flat on his chest, physically preventing him from hitting the Asians before he accepted that no more punches could be thrown. It was at least 2 minutes before he finally backed down and, still shouting abuse, walked off.

I don't know what happened to the Asian men. I did not take my eyes off the antagonist as he departed. But I was left shaking. The charity shop manager was standing in the doorway. He asked me if I was all right, did I need anything? I could not think of what to say, except, 'Please could I have that copy of *Eighteenth-Century Exeter*?'

When did I take the decision to get involved? It wasn't instantly. It was when the white man headbutted the Asian chap and everything suddenly seemed more dangerous. But the decision was itself a sort of very rapid evolution of thought. As far as I can remember, the process was as follows. *This is getting ugly. It could be stopped. It should be stopped. No one else is going to try and stop it. But I am not a strong man. What do I do? Am I the sort of person who stands by and watches this happen right in front of him? I don't want to be someone who does nothing while things go from bad to worse. Remember those 50 New Year's resolutions – if I had known this fight was going to happen at the start of the year, would I have resolved to stand by and watch? Or would I have resolved to try to stop it? What sort of man am I? And if the answer to that is 'someone too scared to get involved', is that really the sort of man I want to be?*

That is the fundamental question, which is probably the beating heart of this book. What sort of person do you really want to be? The answer is not simply something you decide. It evolves in your mind. This is a truth I have learned from running, and from the thousands of decisions that go into turning the choice to run into a result with which you are satisfied. You can't change *who* you are but you can change *what* you are – in the sense that you can choose how and when you act. You can make commitments that will make you feel proud and glad – or you can fail to make them. In doing so, in choosing to make them, you don't just give yourself the ability to commit yourself further, you force yourself to do so. It becomes unavoidable. In the case of Sophie's grandfather, that entailed carrying a wounded man up the Normandy beaches under the fire of German machine-guns. In my case, it meant stopping a hysterical man from carrying out a racially charged act of violence on the streets of Exeter. But it all begins with the choice to get involved – to enter the race in the first place, to stick with the man on your shoulder and to sprint for the line. Or, to put it another way, to become the author of your own story.

Later I discovered that 230 people ran today. I was in the top 5 per cent. And doesn't that detail appear trivial now?

36 | THE HEART OF THINGS

18 November

Romance takes me to the north coast of Norfolk this week. Our neighbours and good friends Simone and Rob are getting married. They have scheduled the ceremony for a Saturday afternoon, which leaves me the morning in which to do the parkrun at nearby Holkham Hall, the eighteenth-century seat of Thomas Coke, Earl of Leicester. Driving through the park in the bright winter light, the Palladian building strikes me as elegant, at least from the outside, glowing golden with the morning sun on its sand-coloured stone. I turn to look across the lake and the park, designed by the great landscape architect William Kent.

This is a wonderful place for a run.

I jog to keep warm as other runners arrive. The overnight frost has put many of them off: only 83 are joining me. I try to pick out the most athletic-looking. A man and a woman are already standing on the start line, chatting and laughing. Both in their thirties, dressed in slick black gear, they are definitely contenders. A chap in his twenties with long orange socks is pacing up and down by the lake. There's a tall man dressed in blue, who looks as though he could be fast. We listen to the announcements from the run director, and hear how this is an 'undulating, mostly uphill' course for the first half, and a gentle downhill one for the return.

As I guessed, the man and woman on the front row head off faster than everyone else. I follow immediately behind them, running along the path and over the grass, through a gate beside a cattle grid and onto the long, rough track that is the first half of the course. After a mile, I am still in third despite the loose stones and the upward slope of the path. My pace is not that fast but, all things being considered, I am quite pleased.

A little further on, I hear someone behind me. As we near the halfway mark, the young man with orange socks appears on my left. Much to my surprise, he starts up a conversation. I can barely respond. Clearly this pace is much easier for him than it is for me. When we approach a magnificent column at the top of a slight incline, I splutter my apology for not being able to keep up with him. 'See you at the finish,' I shout as he pulls ahead. I puff on up to the monument and start to descend towards the stately home. I hear more footsteps. The low sun behind me casts two shadows across the road surface. I put on a bit of speed. One man decisively overtakes me; the other falls back. I cross the line in fifth place, followed home by a young lad.

Reflecting on the run, I am conscious of how little I saw of it. It could have been just the six of us running for all I knew, not 84. Sometimes those at the front have no idea about the following pack. This strikes me as a powerful metaphor for society. It is reminiscent of how leaders know very little about what it's like to be poor and disempowered. Men like Thomas Coke would have known as little about his tenants' budgets as your average billionaire today knows about the price of milk. But this ignorance goes both ways. Those who dug that lake for the earl in the eighteenth century would have had very little idea of his worries, such as his losses on the stock market and the bad behaviour of his only son and heir, and that son's loveless marriage which guaranteed there would be no dynasty. The truth is that if you want to know what is going on, the place to be is right in the middle of things. There, you have an awareness of what matters to the majority, even if you are only just vaguely in touch with the elite and those at the back.

This realisation quickly leads to another: that the best spot for a writer to observe everything is definitely the middle. You don't want to be too rich or too poor. Not too northern nor too southern. Not too urban or too rural. Shakespeare came from just such a place, socially and geographically. He was the son of an alderman of middling wealth in Stratford-upon-Avon: a small town in the Midlands. Of course, not all great writers fit this blueprint. These days especially, when more than four-fifths of the population live in a large town, most people are not born within easy reach of the fields, as Shakespeare was, and thus do not know the natural world as intimately as he did. But my point is that growing up in the middle of society not only allows you to see what is happening more clearly but also gives you the best chance of getting on with other people, regardless of their background. To paraphrase the great man himself, you can walk with kings without losing the common touch.

In my case, I should be grateful that I was born the son of an architect who worked for the council. In addition, I should be grateful that both my parents were familiar with both town and country ways, with the result that I was raised between London, Dartmoor and the South Downs. I feel equally at home in a city, a village or the wilderness. The only thing that alienates me from some people is that I had a first-rate education. Even my own children think I'm a little odd when I tell them they should look forward to their exams because they are a chance to show off. On the whole, being in the middle of things has served me well. And that even goes for writing about running. Would my thoughts mean as much if I was always out in front? Probably not. I'd be more focused on personal success than exploring these insights. Similarly, would I be able to write about the experiences of the ordinary man and woman over the centuries if I had grown up as the heir to a stately home like Holkham Hall? Again, probably not. I have to be grateful that I was not handed everything on a plate, and that I have had to struggle at times. Without the understanding that follows from that, I would not be a writer at all.

37 | ENDURANCE

23 November

Do you have a dog? If so, you'll know just from throwing a ball that man's best friend can outrun you. If you have a cat, you'll be aware that there's no way you can chase it all the way down the garden because your furry companion is so much faster. It has to be said that human beings make very bad sprinters compared to other animals. Cheetahs can run at 70 mph, which is very impressive compared to my puny 14 mph over 200 metres. Even Usain Bolt's world record for the 100 metres – 9.58 seconds – is only 28.9 mph, which is barely a post-prandial stroll for your average cheetah. But cheetahs don't do long runs. Nor do domestic cats. Neither do most dogs. Huskies are unusual in that they can run for very long distances but only in the Arctic, where they don't overheat. As for our closest evolutionary relatives, chimpanzees, their buttocks are insufficiently developed to allow them to run for great distances. Early hominids were similarly lean in the gluteus maximus department. The longer the distance, the better adapted we big-bottomed humans are to outrunning other animals. Only a handful of creatures, such as ostriches, camels and pronghorn antelopes can keep up speeds faster than humans over 20 miles.

Ah, but what about horses, you say. A man cannot outrun a horse over any distance. Well, that is not entirely true. Elite runners *can* beat horses over long distances – as shown by the Man versus Horse Marathon in Wales. Okay, the horses have to carry riders and, yes, they do still normally win. But men do occasionally beat the leading horse over the 22-mile course. In Prescott, Arizona, there are the 25-mile and 50-mile Man Against Horse races up and down a mountain. Here too the horses have to carry riders – they wouldn't be so stupid as to run up a mountain otherwise – and they do often win. But not always. In 1995, Paul Bonnett became the first runner to beat all the horses in the 50-mile race. The feat was repeated in 2001 by Dennis Poolheco, when he won in 6 hours and 33 minutes. It's rare that a horse manages to cover the course faster than that.

I am not about to try to outrun a horse. My point is rather that endurance is one of our greatest qualities. We persevere at things. This doesn't just apply to running, of course. A little over 30 years ago, a lecturer in American Literature at Exeter University, Ron Tamplin, gave me some very good advice. 'Being a writer is easy,' he said. 'All you need is a pen and paper – and the determination to keep at it until something forces you to stop.' He was right. The philosophy of 'keep at it' is one of the reasons I'm a writer today. There are many people with more ability than me but relatively few of them keep at it long enough to develop a literary voice. Of course, Ron could have made this observation about keeping at it 'until something forces you to stop' for a great many activities. It is why my aunt, Angela Mortimer, won her three Grand Slam singles tennis titles, including Wimbledon. 'She would hit the ball against the garage wall until the garage wall couldn't take it any longer,' my father used to say. Success in so many areas of life depends on endurance. Brain surgery is one of the few that doesn't. At least, I hope you don't become a brain surgeon simply by 'keeping at it'.

So why bring up the subject of endurance? The reason is that the end of the year is approaching and I haven't completed my fifth half marathon. I went online and searched for one last week but they are all fully booked. It seems the whole country has gone half-marathon-mad. This leaves me two options. First, I could give up on the idea and blame everyone else for keeping me from fulfilling that New Year's resolution. Or I could do what I said I'd do earlier in the year and run a marathon instead.

Now, a marathon is not something to be taken lightly. I haven't forgotten that I was delirious and feeling sick at the end of the Great West Run, a mere 13.1 miles, so what will I be like after 26.2? However, I was encouraged by that long run along memory lane that I did in Bromley a couple of weeks ago. If I can manage 19 miles without too much misery, then surely I can work my way up to doing 26.2 over the next 3 weeks? I now have running shorts that will not rip my thighs to shreds. So I have taken the plunge.

I have entered the Portsmouth Marathon. It will take place on Sunday 17 December.

In the meantime, it seems a good idea to do some training. Not even I believe I can run a marathon without some idea of what is in store. Oliver does, bless him. He and Alexander exchanged words over the dinner table last night when I told them of my plan.

'Anyone who thinks they can run a marathon without at least four months' training is completely mad,' declared Alexander.

'But you're forgetting one thing,' replied Oliver. 'Dad isn't just anyone.'

Oh, Oliver, bless you! Such faith in my ability not only gives me confidence, it spurs me on. Alexander is right, of course, but his reality check only puts me off. Your confidence makes me want to succeed.

―――――――――

In the middle of Dartmoor is a place called Two Bridges. It is literally a pair of road bridges side by side over the West Dart River, about 12.5 miles from my house. There and back will thus amount to a 25-mile run, almost the full distance of a marathon. On top of this, some of the hills are steep and demanding; the first 5 miles in particular see the road climb about 300 metres (1,000 feet). But I am undaunted. I will just keep to an 'I could do this all day' sort of pace, and do my best.

It is glorious in the sun, although a bit windy, and I coast along quite easily. But climbing up onto the high moor I do begin to wonder. The constant climbing is causing pain in my pelvis. And the wind is brutal, hard in my face. I am sweating and my brow is being blown dry almost instantly. The wind is actually the remains of Hurricane Ophelia: it is so strong that several times I trip as my right leg is blown hard into the path of my left one when it is off the ground.

I make it up all the hills and jog past the Warren House Inn. This is the 6.6-mile mark, a quarter of the marathon distance, and I am already a good deal more than a quarter exhausted. I can see Bellever Tor, standing high and beautiful in the centre of the moor, and tell myself that today I am going to run beyond that. On I go, pushing myself into the wind, which is buffeting my ears with a constant roar. I wipe my face and it feels as if it is covered in very fine sand. I lick my fingers: it is salt from my dried sweat. I limit my steps to short paces as I descend the long hill into Postbridge, not wanting to damage my bones, grateful to be out of the wind. But I know that that slope is going to be very hard to climb on the way back. I cross the East Dart River beside the famous old clapper bridge and start a slow climb to Bellever Forest. From here it is relatively steady all the way to Two Bridges: along to the Cherrybrook, past the ruins of the gunpowder mill and then beneath Crockern Tor before descending to the West Dart River. I reach Two Bridges in just under 2 hours and cross the river by one bridge and return by way of the other, to start the homeward run.

All is still going well at 14 miles. But then, suddenly, I don't feel so strong. I push on past Hairy Hands Corner, where motorists claim occasionally to have seen disembodied hairy fists wrenching the steering wheel out of their control: these are supposedly ghostly hands from the gunpowder mill. I climb the hill on the far side and remind myself that it is steady from here to Postbridge. But I myself don't feel that steady. My watch tells me I have done 16.5 miles, so there are only 2 miles more back to the Warren House Inn. I slog up the hill but then, about 100 metres from the top, I just can't find the energy to do it. Not even the wind, which is now pushing me from behind, can encourage me to keep going. I walk up, my leg muscles crying out with pain. It is a blessed relief to start running again at the top, to pass the Warren House and complete the 19th mile. But now I am ascending the side of Birch Tor, and it is hard. Once more I have to stop and walk, and again it is painful to do so. When I start running again my legs feel grateful but my entire body is devoid of energy.

I just can't do this.

I jog in agony down a hill, my legs aching with every step. I cross a brook and push on, up the next slope. I am fantasising about milk, how cool and white it is. I want some so much! I think too about cider, dry cider. *There is some in the utility room, Ian, you can have it when you get home.* I start dreaming of sipping orange juice... *There is some beside your desk.* I wish I had brought a drink of some sort with me. I am exhausted, dehydrated and disappointed in myself. I come to another hill – and, again, I have to walk up the last section. From the summit, I can see Moreton, just 5 miles away. Now I am stepping gingerly over the cattle grid, leaving the high moor. But I am all spent. Done in. I cannot run any further. I cannot even run downhill, it is too painful. I make myself carry on to the end of the road and stop. I have run 21.63 miles in 3:28:17. I feel ill and in pain. But it isn't real pain: it's a sort of physical failure. I can't walk, I can only stumble. It starts to rain and I just wish it would rain really hard so I could cup my hands and get a sip of water. All I get is a light shower.

I have never in my life voluntarily made myself feel so much discomfort. Not even when running the Bath Half.

It's good not to be aware of your limitations, I wrote earlier in the year. Today I ran straight into them, as if they were a rugby scrum of grinning Tasmanian devils. I practically invited them to beat me to a pulp. The experience leaves me with real doubts about what I have let myself in for. The Portsmouth Marathon might be flat but some of it is on rough ground and it is 4.5 miles further than I was able to run today on tarmac. But how disappointed will Oliver be if I fail? It is quite a responsibility, to live up to his great faith in me.

Endurance, as I said above, is one of the greatest human qualities. It means simply not giving in. So, I must treat today as a temporary setback, and dig deeper.

38 | OLD AGE

25 November

When does 'old age' begin? You'd be surprised how often I get asked that question. Audiences are generally aware that people in previous centuries died at much younger ages than we do today, so they often ask me about old age. I tell them that life expectancy at birth occasionally sank as low as the mid-twenties, and rose to the dizzy age of forty once or twice in the late sixteenth century, but generally was in the thirties until the nineteenth century. Even then there were times and places where it was very low: the average age of burial in Liverpool in the 1830s was just seventeen. It has only been consistently above fifty in the UK since the early twentieth century. On the other hand, it isn't hard to find medieval and Tudor people who lived to be a hundred. St Gilbert of Sempringham was about 106 when he ascended the heavenly staircase in 1190; Sir John de Sully was 102 when he was excused from giving evidence in a court case in 1386; and Alice George told the philosopher John Locke that she was 108 when they met in 1681, and she lived for another 11 years. But there were many fewer old people in the past than there are today.

So, when does old age begin, if the vast majority of people don't make it to sixty? That age? Younger?

As I've mentioned, my father died at fifty-eight. But he was old before that. His disease dragged him down for the last 10 years of his life, so that he could not do many of the things that we presume middle-aged people can manage without difficulty. In marked contrast, there are men and women who can run marathons in their eighties. The extraordinary Fauja Singh ran the London Marathon at the age of 101. With all this variation, I tend to reach for a standard form of defining old age, if only for the sake of having something interesting to say when I get asked the question 'How old is *old*?' I reply, 'It is the point at which it is more likely than not that you will die before your next birthday.' This changes over the centuries, of course. It also takes into consideration aspects of health and lifestyle. If you are a heavy smoker and don't do any exercise, by this definition you are going to grow old at a much younger age than a non-smoker who runs 30 miles a week. However, laying such personal factors aside, when do you think the average person is more likely to die before they can put one more candle on the cake?

Eighty-five?
  Ninety?
    Ninety-five?

Guess the number and then turn over the page...

102!

Amazingly, at the age of ninety-nine the likelihood of *not* making a hundred is still only one in three. Of course, whether you can still run anywhere when you are 102 is a different matter but, nevertheless, this is one of those statistics that certainly is a reason for optimism.

Young Bob Small is a mere seventy today. To celebrate the fact, Alexander, Oliver and I are heading down to Parke to join him in a parkrun on his birthday. I'm not actually running myself because I need to notch up at least another session as a volunteer before the end of the year, and I also have to head off to York immediately afterwards to give a lecture, but the boys will both be taking part, as will many of our friends.

At Parke I am marshalling in my usual place by the bridge at about the 3K mark when the leader charges past me for the first time. A minute after him comes the second runner, with the third in hot pursuit. Then they start to come thick and fast. Everybody's legs and clothes are streaked with mud. The first time Alexander passes me he is running in twentieth place. Not far behind him is Mike Peace, who is one of the 'Ever-Presents' – the 11 runners who have completed every single London Marathon since the first one, in 1981. He's now sixty-eight and ran this year's London Marathon in 3 hours and 58 minutes, which I find extraordinary. As always, Mike thanks me profusely for my marshalling – no mere thumbs up from him. Then I see Oliver, who is just ahead of Bob. But the birthday boy catches Oliver on the old railway line and when I next see them, the order is reversed. Eventually the tail runner passes me, and I nip up to the café, hand Bob his birthday present, and ask him about his run.

'To be honest, Ian, when you get to seventy, it's not so much about how fast you go. I wasn't feeling too well today. But it's like you say, "Leave no race unrun." And in that sense, it was a victory. That's what I call it anyway. Because that is what I feel every time I toe the starting line.'

———————

I am on the train to York when the results come through. Bob finished sixty-third, not his best performance. But his age grade today was 64.79 per cent, which is as good as I've ever done at Parke. I wonder how it compares with other people's efforts. Top of the pile today with 70.25 per cent is a woman in her twenties. Next is a teenage girl (69.44 per cent), then a teenage boy (68.61 per cent). Fifth is Mike Peace (68 per cent). Bob's age grade is the tenth-highest, which is pretty good when you are not feeling well.

I find myself wondering what society would be like if running were not the only thing that was age-graded. Imagine, for example, that money was age-graded too, so that Bob's £1 would buy three pints of milk whereas mine would only buy two. As things stand, many things are loaded against older people: a seventy-year-old has to pay 133 per cent as much as a fifty-year-old for car insurance. The young too could benefit from an age-sensitive financial system. People have difficulty saving the deposit to buy a house before they start a family. Human biology dictates that a woman's fertility declines very rapidly in her late thirties but the average first-time buyer these days is aged thirty-two. It's a race against time for many young people to set up home before babies come along. So what about making the price of a new house sensitive to the stage of life of the purchaser?

I know, I know. The problems are overwhelming. With regard to the house purchases, how could you justify paying suppliers and builders less for their goods and services just because the eventual purchaser was under the age of thirty? And what would people think if the young couple decided not to have a family but just wanted a cheap house so they could go on more expensive foreign holidays? An age-graded economy makes for a wonderful dream but would be madness in practice. We do already accommodate some age-related needs within our present system, such as reduced-price admission for pensioners to historical sites and cinemas, student discounts in certain stores, and the cheapness of rail travel for those with a young person's railcard. However, there is a reason why money has the universal power over us that it does, in that its value is derived collectively from all our many and varied needs. The banknote in your pocket represents a universal calibration of values: a democratic consensus as to what things are worth. Start playing around with that basic principle of collective value and you start creating inflationary and deflationary pressures. You'll also be accused of penalising people on the basis of their age. Since people have no control over how old they are, that is hardly fair.

Having said all these things, money tends not to be so much of an issue for those in their sixties and seventies. I know that there are those for whom that statement does not apply, who are hampered by a limited income – distraught by lack of funds, even – but money seems to be less important for retired people than it is for younger ones. The nineteenth-century politician Joseph Brotherton gave a hint as to why when he said, 'My riches consist not in the extent of my possessions but in the fewness of my wants.' People's wants tend to diminish as they grow older. While in your twenties, thirties and forties, you might well think you could never have enough money to count yourself truly rich, in your fifties you tend to have a more pragmatic view of your financial horizons. In later life you realise that you can achieve a greater sense of wealth simply by not wanting things you don't already have.

As I sit here on the train musing on this point, I realise that Brotherton's great quotation doesn't just apply to money. A mass of positives doesn't necessarily add up to happiness but a complete lack of negatives almost certainly does. If you're still running 5K regularly in your seventies, you may well be keen to run faster each week but the very fact that you're still able to run suggests that you're doing better than most people. If you're hitting the top ranks of the age-grade board, as Bob Small and Mike Peace are, then I dare say you are close to being the envy of everyone, regardless of how much money you have. It certainly makes being old a much more attractive prospect: to think that what will truly satisfy you is not the pursuit of riches but simply maintaining 'the fewness of your wants', through regular exercise, sleeping soundly, eating well and generally enjoying life.

So keep on keeping on. What you are doing in running is eliminating a whole area of potential 'wants' that otherwise might impoverish you. It is strange to think that although running won't make you any money, it can still add to your 'riches' in Brotherton's sense of the word. Indeed, multimillionaires may yet be jealous of you.

39 | THE INSPIRATION TO BE INSPIRATIONAL

9 December

Alexander has caught the running bug. At first the signs were subtle, such as his comment that 'parkrun is *so* addictive'. Then there was a phone call from him one afternoon: 'Dad, what do I need to look out for when buying a pair of good running shoes?' On Tuesday last week, he joined me on a jog down the cycle path. Before we set out, I measured his resting pulse. Later, using the worldfitnesslevel.org website (the 4,631 Norwegians), we estimated his VO_2 Max at 61 mL/kg/min. As you know, I don't trust this resource myself but I wanted to make a point to him. I used this statistic to show him that he had the potential to run 5K in 16:48. That left him reeling with the idea that he could possibly come first in a parkrun. You could see all the Christmas lights coming on at once in his eyes. Proof of his conversion came on the Thursday before last. He went out in the dark to run 4.5 miles around the streets of Moreton, sporting a new pair of three-quarter-length leggings he'd purchased that day in Exeter. Another five runs followed over the next 9 days.

The idea of running faster than everyone else has proved to be a far more powerful incentive than the £50 I promised him if he could beat me by the end of the year.

It is cold this morning. When I open the curtains to my study, I see the lawn outside is covered with a thin layer of snow. The trees are stark against a grey sky, which is washed with patches of white cloud. Birds have collected on the roof of the house next door and are swooping down every so often across our garden, or darting up to the bird feeder on our balcony. I sip coffee, not wanting to step outside in the freezing air until the last minute. I can hardly believe that I picked the last winter raspberry off the bushes in the garden just 10 days ago. And it still tasted good.

Oliver is taking part in the Devon Junior Chess Championships today, so he won't be joining us. Andy Gardner has developed an injury, so he too has sent his apologies. Thus just Alexander and I head into Exeter and line up with 257 other runners beside the canal.

The run director counts down to the whistle and Alexander launches himself into the leading pack, in sixth or seventh place. I am caught by a bit of jostling and fall back to make way for a couple of eager runners, and dodge to one side to go past a slower one. Then I set about catching Alexander. After 400 metres I pull alongside him. I think about running past but hesitate. This isn't like our previous runs. This time he is fitter than ever. We are definitely taking part in a race, not just a run. I don't want to leave myself too tired to compete later. Thus we continue to run abreast of each other all the way to the bridge. There Alexander starts to edge ahead. I try to keep in touch but he is pulling away from me. After the first mile, the gap is 10 metres. It is the same distance after the second. A young man overtakes me as we go around the last muddy corner, and then another. Alexander is getting away from me. I thank a marshal and know that Alexander will not have been able to hear me, he is so far ahead. But I can see from his body movement, swinging from side to side with each pace, that he is growing tired. I look at my watch when I get to the midpoint of the bridge – it says 15:31. *If I run my fastest from here to the end, I will finish in about 20:30. Surely he cannot beat that time?* But I can hardly believe he is still ahead of me now. *Okay, Ian, dig deep. You need to run the last three-quarters of a mile in under 5 minutes. You know you can, as you did it last year. Go for it.*

I steadily close the gap. I know that when I pass my son, I must do so decisively. And I must not leave it until too late. If I overtake him within sprinting distance of the finish, he will be able to beat me on the dash for the line. I build my speed. Ten metres between us. He will soon be aware that I am on his shoulder. Five metres. And I sprint. He senses me there and he too starts to sprint. *I am not going to get past him.* I fall back, and now we are running abreast again, as we were at the start of the run. He is not giving in. I need a strategy.

My mind goes back to last night's chess game with Oliver. I made a mistake and was utterly destroyed within five or six moves. 'There's only one word to describe that game,' Oliver declared as he surveyed my checkmated king and scattered surviving pieces. 'Remorseless.' He was right. And now, with only half a mile to go, I need to be remorseless in racing Alexander. It is not a sudden burst of speed I require but a gradual ratcheting up of the pace, putting on the pressure. So that is what I do. We are running faster now than we were at the start. This is hurting. He is coming with me. He holds me off for a few seconds more – but then admits defeat. 'Go for it, Dad!' he shouts. And I am past. I keep the pressure on, imagining him being right behind me. I remember the parkrun in France where he overtook me a few seconds after I managed to pass him. I build my speed still further. It is tough but I just keep going as fast as I can. I sprint for the last 200 metres and cross the line in 20:29. I take my token and turn to see Alexander finishing 5 seconds behind me.

I am ecstatic for him, truly impressed. I tell him so, and hug him. We head off to a café to have doughnuts and coffee to celebrate.

You cannot walk away from witnessing such improvement without reflecting on the inspiration that lies behind it. It is very different from tuition. At no point did I instruct him in what he needed to do to improve his times. Nor did I simply tell him that he could run far faster than me. Instead, I showed him. The inspiration lay in the difference. It's what actors and film directors mean when they say: 'Show, don't tell'. Writers also emphasise this distinction.

Telling someone what to do is not inspiring. However, if you *show* someone what he might achieve, and give him the space or the opportunity to explore how he might get there himself, he may well be inspired.

Just think back over recent weeks. When Oliver declared to Alexander that 'Dad isn't just anyone', he wasn't telling me what I should do, he was showing his faith in me and giving me the opportunity to live up to it. He might not have realised it but that was the case – inspiration doesn't need to be delivered consciously. When I showed Alexander that he is capable of running 5K in less than 17 minutes, I was letting him see that he *could* win races – how he actually sets about doing it is up to him. When Alexander in turn showed me he had improved so much that he could beat my time from last week, he gave me the incentive to perform at a higher level. One by one, we have all inspired each other. It's another example of the virtuous circle at work. Conversely, those who attempt to lead their protégés along a narrow path, or dictate their expectations, are not inspirational. They fail to create the space in which the pupil can develop and succeed.

This, I can see, is why parkrun is so successful. There is no compulsion built into it. As Paul Sinton-Hewitt said, he built a 'playground' in which people can take part if they so wish. But the great thing is that he also built a means by which to target success, and in doing so created the space for people to work out for themselves how to make their hopes a reality. It is not just Alexander who inspires me to try to run faster.

It is knowing that Oliver will be proud of me too. Just as I have inspired Andy Gardner to start running, his response has also inspired me. Alfie Fell likewise has picked up his running shoes again, inspired by the Mortimer family. But we can't take all the credit. Would I run with other people every week if it weren't for parkrun? I cannot honestly say that I would. And without parkrun, I probably would never have written this book. There is inspiration behind our inspiration. I have to doff my cap to Mr Sinton-Hewitt. It is not just that in setting up parkrun he did a good thing. Nor is it simply that he inspired people. His great achievement is to have inspired people to be inspirational themselves. In all the things we might do in life I can't think of anything more admirable than that.

40 | THE MARATHON

17 December

It is cold, 1 degree centigrade, as I sit down on a bench near Southsea Castle and look out to sea. It is perfectly calm and beautiful. The sky is clear and blue with streaks of cloud. Everything is serene. But I am anxious. I am sitting here alone, holding two energy gel sachets, one in each hand, uncertain of whether I should carry them both or just one. They seem so heavy. I decide to zip one in my back pocket and to throw the other away. I want to know I've got a fillip to help me through the twentieth mile. But other than that, it's just down to me.

The dreaded twentieth mile.

Don't think about it, Ian.

Music starts blaring out at the start line, a few hundred metres away. I hear Blondie's 'The Tide is High', followed by Dexy's Midnight Runners' 'Come on Eileen', Culture Club's 'Karma Chameleon' and David Bowie's 'Heroes'. The songs are somewhat predictable and clearly chosen to appeal to people of my generation. Nonetheless, like a worshipper following the Sunday bells to church, I follow the music to the start of the race. Crowds are gathering.

Yesterday I checked the website and saw that just over twelve-hundred runners had registered. There are hundreds with bottles and sachets tucked in their belts. And there are dozens in fancy dress, ranging from Santa Claus costumes to Santa hats and Santa fur-trimmed mini dresses, elves, a Christmas pudding, a 7-foot-high reindeer and an 8-foot-high gingerbread man.

Sophie is planning to come up from Exeter on the train to see me finish. I pray she doesn't see me crossing the line behind a reindeer and a giant Christmas pudding.

A klaxon starts us off. We are away, running along the promenade with the sun-reflecting sea calmly lapping on our right. My plan is to run the first half of the race no faster than 8:30 per mile. After that, it is simply going to be a case of limiting the damage as I naturally slow up. If I can do the first half in 1 hour and 55 minutes and the second in 2 hours and 5 minutes, that will be around the 4-hour mark that every novice marathon runner wants to achieve. But it won't be a disaster if I trundle home an hour after that.

The crowd of runners is slow to thin out. Despite the bunching up, I stick to my planned pace. After 2 miles we come off the beach and run across a bedraggled meadow before coming to a path. Here there is a long queue of people waiting to descend a narrow set of steps onto a muddy beach. Marshals are shouting at us not to jump down the bank. I am stationary for a whole minute, waiting my turn, and then step down onto the shingle and mud. On the far side we clamber up onto a path above the beach and start running in single file. This is slightly frustrating, as we are limited by the speed of the person in front. But then I reflect that this is just as well; I should not be any faster than this.

Some people are running with friends, chatting as they go along. Two men in their thirties are discussing what their wives are up to while they are here. One, who regularly does triathlons as well as marathons, tells the other that his wife is very proud of him for his athletic prowess and will be there at the finish line. The other one's wife can't stand the hanging around and has gone shopping. Gradually I lose touch with their chatter as they move further ahead. New conversations replace them and, in their turn, diminish. Holiday plans. School reports. Bars in Southampton worth visiting. Twice I hear spectators shout, 'Go on, Ian' as they recognise the book covers on my running shirt. Mostly I am concentrating on where I put my feet. The route we are following includes roads, hard paths, shingle beaches, mud, grass and woodland, complete with protruding tree roots. There are thousands of trip hazards. But I look up wherever I can because almost the whole marathon is in sight of the sea. There is something beautifully relaxing about running beside water.

Now we are on to a tarmac path, approaching the quarter-way point. I glance around me: I am surrounded by four female runners, one of them in a red, white and blue top. Everyone at every turn seems to know her: she is called Anna. *Is she famous?* She is certainly the strongest of the four, so I run just behind her. At the seventh mile, I start to feel a pain in my pelvis, the same pain I felt ascending the hills on the Two Bridges run. I try to put it out of my mind. I think of another Anna, my first sweetheart from Petts Wood. *I wonder where she is now.* Our pace varies according to the terrain. The grass is rapidly turning into a quagmire. There are stiles to negotiate, and sharp turns. But I keep to within 15 seconds of my target pace. At the 10-mile mark, Anna stops to hand her gloves to someone in the crowd. But very soon she catches up with me – and this time she goes ahead. I think of trying to stay with her but I restrain myself. Better to stick to my plan, bearing in mind how hard the later stages of this race are going to be.

We're on Hayling Island now, running along wet paths and through large puddles. I see the race leader coming back from the halfway mark. Ten seconds later, the second-placed man appears. About a minute after that, the rest start to come through – in twos and threes at first and then in clusters, and then in a stream. I slip all over the place but still I am keeping within 10 seconds of 8:30 per mile. I look at the returning runners. There is a young woman dressed as Santa, in a short red dress; there is the 7-foot reindeer costume that I saw at the start; and there is Anna, who is smiling. In running behind her for 4 miles I never once saw her face. And then she is gone.

When I myself reach the halfway mark I glance at my watch and see I've actually covered 13.35 miles, so this is going to be longer than the established marathon distance. I grab a drink and start the return. The ground is even more slippery on this side. A woman with long blonde hair in a ponytail goes past me, as do about three or four men. My fourteenth mile is up: 8:51. *Well, that's not so bad, considering the slippery ground...* And I'm still feeling pretty good. The next 2 miles see me back under 8:40 per mile. I overtake the man in the Rudolph suit. I overtake all the men who went past me just after the halfway mark. And as I do so, I realise no one has overtaken *me* for a long time. Of all those who have passed me since the halfway mark, the girl with the ponytail is the only one still ahead. And I can see her. Gradually I close the distance. And overtake.

We're off Hayling Island now, 10 miles to go, and this is feeling good. I am targeting people and aiming to pass them all. There is the girl in the Santa Claus mini dress: I set my sights on her and go past. The seventeenth mile sees me cross the bridge and turn onto very slippery grass and mud, and a twisting path, but this is no problem. I am feeling strong. Ahead are the two friends who were nattering to each other about their wives early on in the race. One of them is having a tough time, the other doing all he can to coax him along. I offer some words of encouragement to the slower man but he can't speak. His friend, however, starts chatting to me, and before I run ahead, we exchange some pleasantries and wish each other well.

Eighteen miles are up. This is going far better than I ever imagined it would. A mile later, my watch buzzes to tell me that I am still doing 8:30 per mile. No one has passed me now for ages, and I am beginning to feel... well, what is the word? Energised? No, more than that. Glorious? No, close but not quite. But, it is a sort of glory. It feels like I am in a state of gloriousness. Yes, this is a gloriousness. I know that that isn't good English but, damn it, 'gloriousness' is just the word. I am chasing down people gleefully, and overtaking everyone in sight. *If this is the only marathon you ever run, make it count. Make it as good as you could possibly do.*

I do not fear the twentieth mile as I thought I would. Quite the opposite: I am thrilled at the prospect of overtaking the long line of people on the path ahead. I close up on them steadily. Those who have earphones have no idea that I am trying to overtake, and I have to call out so they can make space for me to pass. My pace for the dreaded twentieth is 8:18. *Oh, wow! Didn't my pelvis ache earlier? I can't remember.* This is even better than that long run in early November, revisiting the places of my youth. It reminds me of driving a motorbike along the fast lane of a dual carriageway and simply overtaking everyone at will. In fact, it is exactly like that. My twenty-first mile is up: 8:09. *That's fantastic! But you know what, Ian? You can run even faster. Go on!* As we come close to another single-file path beside the water I see everyone ahead running far too slowly and leap up onto the narrow waterfront wall. I see a chap ahead swinging his arms wildly. 'Coming up on your outside,' I shout, and dash past him. Back on the grass, I see more people to overtake. This is simply an amazing feeling. People talk about hitting a wall in the latter stages of a marathon but I have hit a red carpet. No one has overtaken me since the halfway mark. *Keep it that way, Ian, all the way to the finish.*

I am running easily now, looking at the view across the water. It is as if I am in a dream. It is the most sublime, beautiful feeling. I am passing people so positively that they are shouting encouragement to me. A young woman in a club shirt shouts, 'Good on you!' as I run past her. 'Thank you,' I shout back, lifted still higher. Twenty-four miles are up. I've never run this far in my life before and yet it is so natural. It is far easier than all those half marathons I laboured over earlier in the year. What was it that Emil Zatopek said? 'Pain is a merciful thing – if it lasts without interruption, it dulls itself.' I have never believed that. When I have quoted it in the past, I have always added, 'if it lasts without interruption, it is dulled by the boredom'. But this is not boring at all – it is exhilarating. The sheer joy of this race is making every muscle in my body tingle with excitement.

I am running at 7:50 per mile now. I have no pain at all, no desire to stop.

Oh, wonder of wonders! Do other people feel this euphoria, this rejoicing? It does feel tremendously physical, sexual and invigorating. I know it is predictable and perhaps a little vulgar – so I apologise for this – but I can't help comparing the experience with sex as I head to the end, faster and faster. That thought makes me chuckle as I run. I cannot remember anyone ever talking about long-distance running to me in terms of physical passion but that is what it is like now. I told Sophie that this is the one and only marathon I will ever run. But can I honestly say I will never do this again? Maybe I will have to slip out of the house discreetly, or go on a furtive trip – to have a secret liaison with a 26-mile-long mistress.

Here we are back on the promenade, a fast surface. I know that the finish line is still a way off – but that is a good thing, because I don't want this to end. Not yet. I am running at 7:36 per mile and everyone I see ahead is either running slowly or walking. I am like a little boy playing Superman, swooping past them all in the playground. David Bowie's 'Heroes' is now blaring out in my mind, just for me. This moment is unrepeatable. Never again will I embark on a run and be so taken by surprise at how well it goes. If I were to enter another marathon, I would have expectations. The unexpectedness of it all is part of the gloriousness.

I can see the pier now, which is just this side of the finish. It starts raining but I don't care. I am singing the 'Ode to Joy' from Beethoven's 'Choral' symphony, and remembering why I started running in the first place. On the day after what would have been my father's eightieth birthday, had he lived, I had difficulty getting out of bed because I was 3 stone overweight. 'My father would not have wanted this for me,' I said to myself that day. 'He would have wanted me to take charge of my life.' For a moment I feel a few tears welling up in my eyes as I remember him. Raindrops fall on my face. But this is no time for sadness. My father would be proud if he could see me now. Look, there are still three people left this side of the line. *Two will be easy to reach but can you catch the third?* And I sprint. Full of joy for life, and my memories, and my family, I run hard. I push myself as fast as I can go. This is it. This is what life is all about: joy, desire, competition, homecoming, speed, exuberance, physicality, triumph and fulfilment. And with a final determined effort, I run past that third person, and cross the line.

Sophie comes over to me and gives me a kiss. 'You've done it!' she exclaims. 'Good thing I caught a taxi from the station. If I'd walked as planned, I'd have missed you.' She hands me a Lucozade Sport. Bless her. I sit on the ground and taste it, and feel very, very happy.

There is something squidgy in my back pocket.

It's that energy gel.

As we walk away, I can't stop talking about the run. It's not so much that I want her to know all about it but rather that I don't want to break the spell. This has been one of the best experiences of my life. I want to be in this euphoric state, looking forward to the end, forever. In the same way I want to be anticipating my sons running faster than me, forever. Just for once everything has gone right. It is a golden moment.

Later, when I have time to consider the results, I see that I came 152nd out of 879 finishers. My official time is 3:48:12, exactly an hour and a minute behind the winner. Strava tells me that my time for the actual marathon distance of 26.2 miles was 3:41:30, and at the end as I passed that last runner, I was doing 6:18 per mile. I was prepared for this day to be all about suffering, endurance and gritted teeth. Although I quietly hoped to break 4 hours I never imagined I'd run the second half of the race faster than the first. Finishing in the top 20 per cent of my first marathon feels like a triumph. I beat my self-doubts. I overtook them in that twentieth mile.

What is the meaning of all this? I'm tempted to say, 'Who cares? Euphoria does not need to have meaning.' However, such an experience contains many lessons. The first is very simple: extraordinary things *do* happen. Every once in a while, everything *will* go right. I strongly suspect that, in this case, the lack of pressure had something to do with it. No one was expecting me to finish in under 4 hours. There were people to support me along the way: strangers, bystanders who recognised the book covers on my shirt, runners to whom I spoke or who shouted their encouragement as we neared the end, and even people with whom I never exchanged a word, like Anna. That club runner who shouted out, 'Good on you!' as I overtook her particularly sticks in my memory. She made me feel proud. Somehow, accidentally, everything came together. I created the right conditions for success – and it happened.

Driving home, I remember that old man who spoke to my father after I defeated him in the only race we ever had, which I mentioned in chapter 27. His words that day were 'This is when you know you're getting old'. How wrong, how *utterly* wrong, he was! It doesn't matter if Alexander overtakes me next Saturday or not. My ageing has got nothing to do with him or anyone else. How can my being overtaken by my son be a mark of 'getting old' if at the same time I am discovering new states of euphoria? Exploring new worlds, breaking new ground? If this is 'getting old', bring it on! Give me more races to run, more mountains to climb, more candles to burn, more wine cellars to empty, more unexpected, sweet conquests. Let no race be unrun! Let me embrace the world!

After all, I'm not going to be 102 for another five decades.

41 | THE SHOWDOWN

23 December

I have slept very badly but am up at 7 a.m., while it is still dark. I make Sophie a cup of tea, let the cats out and do some reading before waking the others. One by one they appear. Elizabeth goes from her bedroom to bathroom with a great crashing of doors – how is it that teenagers can close doors with more noise than anyone else? Oliver stumbles down the stairs, grunts 'good morning', and makes his way to the fridge for a yoghurt. Alexander blearily comes into my study wearing odd socks. I point this out to him. 'I know,' he replies. 'It's for the greater good.' Then he goes out again.

Moreton is wreathed in mist but as we drive down the Wray Valley, towards Parke, the sun breaks through. This has the magical effect of gilding the atmosphere through the trees on either side of us, giving the air a pink glow. Every so often we break out of the fog and are hit by the full glare of the sun, flashing straight into our eyes and glinting off wet granite and twigs on either side of the car. A few moments later we are once again surrounded by the Tolkienesque mistiness, with crooked tree branches and tumbledown walls on both sides of the valley, and high hills towering above us.

On arrival at Parke, Oliver heads off to take up his position as marshal, and Alexander and I take our places amongst the runners. Two hundred people have turned up. 'Where are your Santa costumes?' one of the organisers says, as many of the runners are sporting a bit of festive garb, whether it be a piece of tinsel, a hat or the full Santa suit. In truth, dressing up didn't even cross my mind: I was preoccupied with thinking about Alexander. I have a plan to surprise him – by running out fast and trying to lead from the front. So I make our excuses with a smile and wait for the run to begin.

No one counts down to the start. A whistle goes without warning, and we all suddenly realise we are meant to start running. It wrongfoots me. Alexander charges off and I have no hope of getting in front of him, so that's my plan blown straight away. Not that it stood much chance of success. I don't feel very energetic. He is in about tenth place as we descend the rocky slope towards the gate. I am six places behind him. It is terribly muddy; I don't relish the slipperiness and I know I am running cautiously. As we go through the gate and start the 1-in-4 climb up through the woods, I feel very weary. Several people overtake me. I look up: Alexander is leaping up this hill far faster than I can. Perhaps this is the day that he does beat me? *No, Ian, your body will wake up soon.* I work on closing the gap as we run through the woods. Gradually it comes down to about

40 metres. But there it remains. Every time I manage to get within 30 metres I see him pulling away again. As we splash our way back through the middle of the course and head to the bridge, where Oliver is marshalling, Alexander is about 60 metres ahead. I know he doesn't like the long straight of the old railway track, which is the next section, so I hope to reclaim some lost ground there. But although I push hard, so does he. I see him turn to the right and ascend the second hill to the woodland path. I try hard but cannot force my body to go faster.

This is so different from the second half of the marathon, 6 days ago, when my legs responded to every demand. Now they are rebelling, refusing to listen to me.

Down the slope and back onto the old railway line. I throw caution to the wind and charge down the incline. But when I turn the corner, I see Alexander is way ahead. He must have run down the slope even faster. *It is now or never, Ian. Push hard.* I swing my arms more, lengthen my stride and force myself to speed up. I close the gap between us to about 30 metres again. But I cannot get any closer. As we return to the bridge and Oliver shouts, 'Well done, Dad!' I see Alexander giving it all he has got.

I am not going to catch him.

I look to my left. The sun is beautiful across the parkland. It is a good day to accept the inevitable. Everyone is happy because of Christmas. Alexander has beaten me, fair and square.

And now I can stop worrying.

I cross the line and look for him. He is bent over, standing by his mother and sister. I run over and he straightens up. I hug him. And I hold him. The last few months flash through my mind. I think about his taking up the challenge and training almost every day, and his massive improvement over the last few weeks. I know he has learned that if he sets his mind to do something, he can achieve things that he did not think were within his grasp. I know he is exultant. And I just close my eyes and hold him, my precious son.

'So proud of you, Alexander.'

'Proud of you too, Dad.'

'You don't need to be proud of me.'

'No. But I am anyway.'

I was the first person ever to hold him, at the moment of his birth, almost 19 years ago. And now, look how far we've come. How good the journey has been. How bright the view from this newly conquered summit.

Sometimes losing can feel like victory.

I take some chocolate from the box proffered at the finish line and walk back down to where Oliver is marshalling. I am thoughtful all the way. It has finally happened. And it is a relief. I no longer have to be apprehensive. I don't just mean about Alexander beating me; I mean about life in general – and turning fifty in particular. As I approach the place where Oliver is doing his duty, I hear him clapping every single runner who passes, saying to them all, 'Well done' or 'Keep it up, it's not far to go now.' For a lad who does not talk much, it gladdens my heart to see him voluntarily speaking to strangers – and not just speaking but encouraging them. Handing him some chocolate, I join him in congratulating and applauding everyone still going – the slow runners who want to get fit; the overweight runners for whom running 3 miles is a physical struggle; those with young children; the old runners who pick their way gingerly over the uneven stones. 'Merry Christmas,' many of them reply. 'Thank you for volunteering.'

———————

Half an hour later we are in the café. The times have come through: Alexander was twenty-first in a time of 22:50. It marks an incredible improvement over the course of 12 months: on Christmas Eve last year he was 121st. His best at that point was 27:17.

'So now you've beaten your dad, what are your targets for next year?' asks Bob Small, who has joined us at our table.

'Keep beating him,' replies Alexander.

'And you, Ian? What does 2018 hold for you, running-wise?'

The question takes me completely by surprise. I don't know what to say. I realise that I have fulfilled my New Year's resolutions as far as running is concerned. I have run 41 parkruns and volunteered at four, so the 45 are complete. My resolution to complete five half marathons was exceeded by one of them being a whole marathon. It will be difficult to top that.

'I'd like to get back to doing 5K in under twenty minutes. That was the ambition this year and I failed to achieve it. So I'll try again in 2018.'

'You don't fancy some of the longer runs? Another marathon?'

'No,' Sophie interjects. 'He doesn't.'

Bob looks at her.

She shrugs. 'I'm just saying it. You know Ian. He'll do what he wants, regardless of what I say.'

Bob turns back to me. 'Well, what about the twenty-mile Granite Way? What do you think – two hours thirty? I think it's the first weekend in March. Or there's a ten-mile course, if you prefer.'

'I imagine Dad will want to get revenge at the next parkrun,' says Alexander.

'I want to run a 10K with Dad,' says Oliver. 'There's one in Plymouth in April. I'll be fifteen then, so I'll be allowed.'

As I listen, it strikes me how those who are nearest and dearest to us are our pacers in life. We all set challenges for each other, and we validate each other's achievements even if we do no more than witness and respect them. And just as the pacer in a race doesn't just set challenges for the person following him but also helps him or her succeed, so too we help each other reach new heights. Up to now I have done this for my sons. From now on, they will do the same for me. They will set the targets and they will encourage me to meet them. Alexander said as much just now, immediately after our race, when he said that he was proud of *me*. I thought at the time that he was merely being polite but now I can see he was acknowledging my role in his triumph. His run today would have meant much less if I had not been there. If I had not done my best to catch him. If I had not put £50 on the table. If I had not embraced him in the moment of his victory over me.

As you know from certain passages in this book, I have always thought that passing the baton to the next generation would be a matter of wistfully watching them run off into the sunset. But now we get to that point, I find it is much more rewarding than that.

They want me to run with them.

42 | THE SKY BENEATH OUR FEET

30 December

Finally we come to the last run of the year. All week we've been talking about it, initially at home in Devon and subsequently in Lewes, where all the family are gathering to celebrate New Year. Alexander is very keen to make sure he beats me today, his nineteenth birthday. He is even more anxious to make sure he is faster than his cousin Tom. Tom, in turn, is eager to overtake me again, to show that last year's result was not a one-off. Oliver is desperate to match his uncle Robbie. For his part, Robbie is determined to conquer 23 minutes. And as for me, I don't care whether Alexander passes me or Tom does, or they both do: I have eyes only for the divine beauty of 20 minutes.

'A runner must run with dreams in his heart, not money in his pocket,' said Emil Zatopek.

Today we are all running with dreams in our hearts.

Conditions are not propitious, however. It has stopped raining and it is not at all cold for this time of year – about 10 degrees – but the wind is strong, 20–25 mph and gusting up to 35 mph, according to the Met Office. On Hove Promenade it is even stronger. A fine mist hangs over the whole beach area: spray from the sea being blown all about, like extremely fine rain. The washed-out sun is trying to break through the clouds but it is only managing to turn the sky into a broad silver glare. The effect, if you look towards it, is eerie: everything in the foreground appears in silhouette, in black and white. Look the other way and everything – people's running gear, the promenade, the grass beyond and the grand houses in the background – all appear in heightened, psychedelic colour.

When the run gets underway, a man in a light-blue shirt heads off fast. Alexander is not far behind him and I am right on his shoulder. But soon a handful of men in their twenties and thirties pass us. The wind is harsh in our faces heading westwards; it roars in our ears and whips tears from our eyes. At the first turn, after about 600 metres, there are four runners bunched right at the front followed by another six, then Alexander, me and then Tom. We embark on the first long straight. I stay with Alexander, right on his shoulder. As we cross the start line again, we are running abreast. He decides to put on a little more speed and goes about 5 metres ahead. I stick with him. But despite the wind now being in our favour, we have only managed 6:25 for the first mile. And now we have to run back straight into the icy blast. We battle against it for the full length of the promenade and, just after the third turn, the second mile comes up. My watch says 7:11. That's it. There's no way we're going to be remotely near my target time. We run the third long straight, pushing hard all the way. On our right, the waves churn over each other in great rolls of grey-green water, sending up spray into our faces. Momentarily I think to myself, I could take it easy, and let Alexander beat me. But then I wonder, would he be running this fast now if I had not set him a target? Likewise Tom. Giving in is not the way to encourage them.

I recall Bob Small asking me last week, what were my running ambitions for 2018. I replied that I wanted to beat 20 minutes. But in saying that, I missed something important. What I really want to do is to encourage Alexander and Oliver and everyone else who runs with us to exceed their expectations. And the way to do that is to set them an example.

A young man in a red shirt passes me. In that instant I make my mind up to run to the end as fast as I can. Just as I have done all year. There is no reason to stop now. Alexander would not want to beat me unless I was giving it everything. I make the last turn a little in front of him and chase after the man in red. He is only a couple of seconds ahead. I increase the pressure on him but he responds positively. I go faster. So does he. Alexander is falling behind us. Tom too has fallen back. I am running alone. I cannot reach the man in red but I push hard all the way nonetheless. I cross the line in twelfth place. When I look at my watch I see it says 21:04. I am hugely disappointed. I turn to see Alexander coming in 5 seconds behind me, and I embrace him. Tom finishes seventeenth in 21:48. Robbie is well outside 23 minutes and Oliver is way behind him.

Every one of us has failed to reach our target – except Alexander, who has at least succeeded in beating Tom.

Oliver is disconsolate and stomps off to stare at the sea. 'That was the worst parkrun ever,' he declares. 'It was absolutely dreadful.'

'It was tough,' I reply. 'But you kept going. You didn't stop. That is what makes me proud of you.'

As we look out at the turbulent water together, I reflect that, just as it is sometimes rough and sometimes calm, so our performances sometimes matter and sometimes don't. Today, for Oliver, it mattered. He wanted so much to run as fast as his uncle. But Christmas festivities, late nights and lack of training did not permit it. When you're in such rough seas the best thing you can do is head for a peaceful bay and calm water. There you can put the turbulence behind you.

———————

Back at my mother's house, I sit down with a cup of coffee and ponder the morning's result. This was not the way it was meant to be. I wanted this last run of the year to be the one when I did my best time, running across the line with my son and my nephew. The message might then have been something along the lines of how we managed to achieve our targets together, how we helped each other. But we didn't even come close.

There were 197 runners at Hove today, so Alexander, Tom and I were all in the fastest 10 per cent. I look for other grounds to be positive. The first man home could only manage 19:11, making this the second-slowest run here in the 2½ years of its history. I was the first finisher aged over fifty, and the second over forty. But such details are small compensation. I cannot now meet my 20-minute target. And what can I say to cheer up Oliver? I feel for him, so angry with himself. I have no doubt he tried his best – yet how can I reassure him that I know that, and that it is all right even though he did not do as well as he hoped?

On the other side of the room hangs a large seascape called *The Sky Beneath our Feet* by the painter Ric Horner, whom I've known since university days. It shows the beach near Whitstable, where he lives, after the tide has gone out. The wet sand is reflecting the wide expanse of the dawn sky except where there are rocks or pieces of driftwood breaking the shoreline. As I look at it, I don't just see the astounding view. I see the sky – the heavens – reflected here on Earth. And that leads me to think that everything you can dream about, everything you can imagine being in a proverbial Heaven, is just a reflection of what we know, here, from day to day.

Earth reflects Heaven, which reflects Earth.

As I continue to stare at the painting, the thought seeps into my mind that all our dreams are really a reflection of reality, and all our realities reflections of our dreams. All the hopes with which we started our run today were aspects of our characters enlarged; they weren't external to us but 'in our hearts'. So it is with life in general. If we can dream of achieving something, then that achievement is already a part of us, for our dreams are only a reflection of what we already are. When I wrote about that fight on the street in Exeter back in November, I suggested that the fundamental question at the heart of this book is 'What sort of person do you really want to be?' I presumed that there is a clear line of distinction between what you are now and that ideal person you want to be. But these two entities are not distinct. They reflect each other. Just as I wanted to be the person who would do the right thing in a situation like that, so my desire reflected what I already was. I just had to find the courage to act.

What an empowering thought that is. In fact, it sounds like the sort of self-improvement talk you get from motivational speakers. However, the more I think about it, the more I see it is true. And for proof, I need only cast my mind back to Oliver today, staring at the churning sea, so upset after 'the worst parkrun ever'. Our dreams are a reflection of what we already are. If they weren't, it wouldn't be so painful when they don't come true.

ENVOI

So there you are. You've had the agony and the ecstasy, the pain and the exhilaration. And you've had a whole series of views on the meaning of running. Why does it matter? Why does *anything* matter? Why do physical fitness, companionship, humour, a fast time, not cheating, pacing yourself, conserving your strength and setting yourself goals matter? And at a deeper level, what does it mean to grow old? Do you know the limits of your determination? How do you cope with failure? And how much do your sons' and daughters' achievements mean to you? Deeper still lies the question of what sort of person you really want to be. If you care about running, even just a little bit, then that point will probably have resonance above all the others. And you will be constantly reviewing and re-examining your answer for the rest of your life.

In looking back over these chapters, I am struck by how little importance I attach to the times I achieved. I said in chapter five that we need times to make sense of our performances. Yes, and at the time they are essential, but how quickly they lose all meaning! Cast your thoughts back to April where I discussed how running reflects aspects of marriage. Perhaps you will recall that Sophie was still asleep when I was on the start line at Parke. But can you remember whether that was a fast run or not? I can't. What about the run at Killerton, when I compared my cliff-falls model of physical decline with the damage to the house: how did I do timewise that day? Again, I can't remember. It doesn't matter. The lessons of these runs have nothing to do with my speed. Indeed, some of the most meaningful experiences came out of my worst performances. The richness of the year depends rather on the people I met, the conversations I had, the relationships with my sons, their physical progress and the adversities I overcame. If I were to choose the piece in this book that means the most to me, I would have to say it is the one when Alexander beat me. I had no idea what I would write that day but, in the end, the recognition that my sons don't think of running off into the sunset without me but want me to run with them opened my eyes to a new world of optimism about growing old. And it all came out of being beaten, fair and square. When you listen to Defeat and Victory lecturing you in the schoolroom of life, it is surprising how often Defeat proves the better teacher of the two.

How many of my New Year's resolutions did I achieve? Thirty-eight, in the final reckoning. Some of the failures were due to matters beyond my control. I was unable to walk 4 miles per day on non-running days when I was recovering from my stress fracture. That also affected my weight. I failed to complete recording my songs with Alexander because he started a part-time job on top of his full-time studies. Other failures were simply down to my lack of perseverance. I did not play my guitar every day. I only took my kayaks out with my sons once – not twice as I had resolved. But 38 resolutions out of the 50 is not bad, especially when I exceeded several targets. As for the great chess tournament with Oliver, after he reached an unassailable 26.5 points, he started playing carelessly and let me win three times, so rather than see him throw away his margin of victory, we called it a day at 26.5 points to 22.5. That resolution was fulfilled in spirit, even if we did not complete all 52 games. On the running front, I covered a total of 811 miles at an average pace of 7:49 per mile. Am I satisfied with that? Yes, considering the injuries I had to deal with, though nowhere near as satisfied as I am with the fact that Oliver conquered me at chess and Alexander beat me at running.

All these things plus the various realisations in the chapters of this book bode well for someone who has hit a certain age and is wondering what the future holds. The best running experiences are going to be those that teach you something beyond the physical dimension, not those in which you register a reasonably fast time. In this sense, ageing is only of minor importance – I'd put it fourth, after (1) what you learn along the way; (2) your greater fitness; and (3) the emotional income you will gain from times you might achieve. This brings me back to the mantra with which I considered beginning this book: 'First you run for fitness. Next you run for speed. Then you run for meaning.' However, after all these experiences, I am not sure that anyone really runs *for* meaning. Just because I find meaning in running does not mean that that is the reason why I run. After all, I find meaning in many things – visiting art galleries, exploring old cities, making love, cooking for the family and drinking wine, to name just a few – but I can't claim that meaningfulness is the reason I choose to undertake any of them. You can do these things gratuitously and have a great deal of pleasure without noticing any significant meanings at all.

What, then, is the driver that makes me sure I will continue to run? If running is a means to an end, what is the 'end' purpose beyond mere fitness and speed?

If you had asked me a year ago I would probably have answered 'self-respect' without thinking too deeply about it. And I don't think that I would have been wrong. Self-respect is incredibly important, as I remarked in chapter nine. Many people run solely for fitness and self-respect, and that is okay. But over the course of the year I have become aware that, for me and many people in a similar position, there is a deeper purpose to running. Now I can feel it, like the wind, blowing through the forest of this book – right from the moment that inspired it. Think back to all the runs when I wanted to stay in bed and got up because of Oliver. Think back to the observation that 'one day I will see gaps between the runners where there used to be sons'.

Remember my running alongside amazing individuals; the question of nature versus nurture; and the inspiration to be inspirational. The majority of the pieces in this book are about our relationships with other people. Consider the last run at Hove, when I decided not to let Alexander beat me but pushed on to encourage him to run even faster, and in so doing realised that my ambitions for next year are not all about me but about encouraging him, Oliver and Tom to run faster – and likewise Andy, Alfie, Bob and anyone else who runs with us. There can be no doubt what my mantra should say.

First you run for fitness. Then you run for speed. Finally, you run for other people.

'I think that's true,' says Alexander, when I mention it at the dinner table. 'There's a parkrun near the university I'm applying to. When October rolls around, I can see you driving up early in the morning and doing a run with me there. A cheeky little 5K.'

'You're not worried I'll beat you?' I tease him. 'In front of your university friends?'

'You won't have a chance. I'm going to carry on training.'

'He'll still beat you on age grading,' Oliver points out to his brother.

'Yeah, he always says that, doesn't he?' Alexander replies. 'Dad will probably have it carved on his tombstone. "Here lies Ian Mortimer – and he still beats Alex on age grading".'

'No,' I say in protest. 'I want my epitaph to say something like "Surely there has been a mistake?"'

'You won't get to choose, Dad,' replies Oliver. 'You'll be dead. Anyway, it's obvious what your tombstone's going to say.'

'What?'

'No run was ever wasted.'

The end

NOTES

1   Thor Gotaas, *Running: A Global History* (London: Reaktion Books, 2009), pp. 78–9.

2   Mark Palmer, 'When David Bedford's patience finally ran out', *Daily Telegraph*, 31 January 2004.

3   This record has subsequently been beaten by Corey Bellemore on 28 October 2017, when he performed a beer mile in 4:33.6.

4   S. Waldek, M.R. Patel, M. Banikazemi, R. Lemay and P. Lee, 'Life expectancy and cause of death in males and females with Fabry disease: findings from the Fabry Registry', *Genetics in Medicine*, 11 (November 2009), pp. 790–6.

5   https://blog.strava.com/the-parkrun-story-paul-sinton-hewitt-8943/

6   https://blog.strava.com/the-parkrun-story-paul-sinton-hewitt-8943/

ACKNOWLEDGEMENTS

A book like this cannot be written except with the help of a large number of people. For a start, I want to thank my agent Georgina Capel and her staff; Lucy York for her editorial work; Julian Beecroft for copyediting; Imogen Palmer for proofreading and Claire Plimmer, Debbie Chapman and the rest of the team at Summersdale. I am significantly in the debt of those who read early drafts of the book and advised me, namely Bob Small, Mary Fawcett, Kate Matheson, Ric Horner, Andy Gardner and Jörg Hensgen. I also want to thank Sarah Pinn, who lovingly tends our garden and created the plentiful fruit that I mention in the summer chapters; and Eleanor Clare, who made the joke about life at fifty being 'a long straight road with death at the end of it', which I quote in chapter 21. Thanks too to Glen Turner from parkrun HQ for comments on chapter 30. My biggest debt is to my wife Sophie, who has been so supportive during the year. I was not the easiest person to live with, apparently, when I was instructed to do no exercise at all in order to recover from my stress fracture. And she was the one who warned me about the damage I might do to myself in attempting a marathon. I hope she forgives me for not following her advice, just as I forgive her for always being right.

In addition to the writing, I would like to thank those who have helped me with the running this year. First and foremost, I am enormously indebted to my sons, Alexander and Oliver, who inspired me throughout. Next, I would also like to thank all those people named in the book, whether as fellow runners, friends or people who simply appeared in my year's narrative. I would especially like to thank my physiotherapist, Mike Ashton, and Jonathan Camp – not only for running the Bath Half with me but also supporting me at Torbay. Thanks too to David, Elizabeth and Sol for support.

Lastly, it would be wrong to overlook all those who have made each event happen. First, I am grateful to the organisers of the Portsmouth Marathon, the Bath Half, the Hereford Half, the Torbay Half Marathon and the Great West Run. But I am sure these good people would not resent me saying I am even more indebted to the many individuals who enable parkruns to happen. None of my runs would have been possible without all the volunteers who give up their valuable Saturday mornings to allow others to run. In the spirit of parkrun, I would like to thank all 599 of them who assisted with the runs described in this book, including a few events that are not described in detail. So here they all are, in order of venue:

Barnstaple (30 Sep): Amber Drake, Barbara Nicol, Beth Woollam, Chris Dent, Dan Hunter, Joshua Simpson, Maggie Jones, Mandy Robbins, Melanie McKenna, Peter Russell, Rachael Dunn, Rachael Hughes, Rick Bond, Sarah Simpson.

Beckenham Place (4 Nov): Ellie Hickman, Emily Pilkington, Gail Arnott, Jane Fawcett, Jenny Hayward, Kyle Davies, Linda Neillands, Maria Chandler, Matt Collins, Pat Kerrins, Paul Booth, Richard Harper, Richard Selway.

Bushy Park (7 Oct): Alex Tickell, Ali Kennedy, Annabelle Sander, Beth Tempest, Brendan Raath, Catelin le Franc, Cleide Burgess, Courtney le Franc, David Stewart, Denise Mitchell, Diane Mullen, Emilie Howes, Ethan Mullen, Ethan Scott, Florence Polwin, Freya Morrison, Helen Carpenter, Helen Edwards, Janice Franks, Jonathan Dickinson, Julie Papworth, Julie Smith, Katrin Kroschinski, Kieron Jake Carpenter, Leonie Kennedy, Lorraine Dillamore, Luca Deacon, Lucy Katesmark, Lucy Thatcher, Mack Downey, Mark Blythe, Melanie Howes, Mike Tivnen, Owen Parry, Pablo Urdiales Antelo, Paul Keddie, Ray Coward, Ray Franks, Robert Morey, Rosie Rendall, Sacha Kennedy, Samantha Fagg, Sarah Connor, Simon Lane, Steve Carpenter, Susan Howarth, Suzanne Green, Toby Davies, Tom Fairbrother, Tracey Lenthall, Wendy Stokes, Yue Man.

Exeter Riverside (7 Jan; 18 Feb; 18 Mar; 22 Apr; 8 Jul; 28 Oct; 2 Dec; 9 Dec): Aby Sampson, Adrian Harding (6), Adrian Mountford (3), Agnieszka Bobon, Ailsa Barrow, Alex Bosley (2), Alex Lupton, Alison Louise Caswell, Andrew Thomas, Anne Devlin (2), Anthony Mott, Babs

Carroll, Barry Lucas (2), Ben Lupton, Bessie Dunn, Caroline Smith, Catherine Mountford (5), Catherine Pragnell, Ceola Wade, Chloe Kershaw, Chris Calvert, Chris James, Chrissie Randall (2), Claire Hadfield, Clare Hardman, Corinne Mcwilliams, Damien Hodge (2), Daniel Mountford, Darren Gallagher, Darren Hutchings, David Wilson, Dee Dowie, Dennis Hall (3), Dianne Goodwin (4), Eleanor Dodd, Emma Kessie, Erica Wright, Eugene Bonner (2), Felicity Ward-Smith (3), Fiona Upton, Francesca Birch, Gail Dennett, Geoffrey Harcombe, Graeme Salisbury (2), Helen Barlow (2), Helena Walker (2), Ivan Jeary, Jack Clutterbuck, Jacob Clark (2), Jan Taylor, Janet Penrose (2), Jenny Lupton, Jilly Scheepers, Jo Pearce (2), John Caswell (3), John Everitt, John Staplehurst (2), Jon Tibbetts, Jonathan Major, Judith Bonner, Julia Batten, Karen Macmillan, Kate Milsom, Katherine Harris, Kayla Rudd, Kelly Lawson, Kubo Macak, Laura Elizabeth Sarson, Laura Jane Sims, Lewis Jones (6), Liana King, Lucy Owen, Lynn Travis, Mark Waddicor (2), Martin Brint (2), Matt Bonne (3), Matthew Bosley, Mike Feighan (2), Naomi Payne, Natalie Johnson, Paul Barter (3), Paul Mouland, Peter Smith, Petra Aubert, Phil Davey (3), Rebecca Barter (6), Richard Ashe (7), Richard Johnson, Richard Stone, Richard Taffler, Robert Andrews (2), Roger Noden, Sarah Ellen Tupper, Sarah Lovell, Sarah Moffat (3), Scott Hunter, Sonia Fielder-Pine (2), Stephen Collier, Steve Hagley, Steven Forrester, Susan Kathleen Noden, Susan Vanden, Terry McWilliams, Tim Lupton, Tom Goffrey, Victoria Butterworth.

Holkham (18 Nov): Adam Skinner, Cat Cameron, Ceridwen Howell, Dave Barber, David Hatherly, David Sharp, Fran Allen, Gail Skinner, Jackie Wrout, Mark Riseborough, Roland Bewick, Susan Riseborough.

Hove Promenade (19 Aug; 23 Sep; 30 Dec): Adrian Heft, Alison Kuy, Andrianna Hadjimichael, Annie Drynan, Antony Bradley (3), Ben Fitzpatrick-Nash, Bev Markham, Carl Bennett, Cass Castleton, Clare Ryan, Dale Smith (2), David Joseph Simmons, Deborah Absalom (2), Dennis Lancaster (2), Georgia Steers (2), Glenn Still (2), Graham Halfacree, Harriet Cunningham, Helen Block, Jackie Ware, Jane Tew (2), Jeff Johnstone (2), Jez Kay, Joanna Lyons, Jon Elsom (2), Karen Bennett (2), Kathryn Martin, Kerry Talmage, Kirsty Pugh, Leah Swallow, Lisa Farmer, Lizzie Elliott, Lucy Dean, Magdalena Strycharska, Mark Brocklehurst (2), Mark Saso, Michelle Pauli (2), Neal Udeen, Niall Roche, Nick Culliss, Nicole Mickey, Nigel Turley, Olle Akesson, Patrick Law, Paul Knott (2), Pete Goodman, Peter Bennett, Peter Ranson (2), Philippa Bull (2), Rachel Dyson (2), Ricky Bennett, Ryan Johnstone, Samuel Bainbridge, Sara Celik (2), Sara Wynne-Potts, Sarah Lewis (2), Simon Steers, Stephen Knott, Stephen Scott, Struan Mackenzie (2), Stuart Roberts, Sue Fallon, Sue Pinnick, Suzy Hawker.

Killerton (21 Jan; 11 Feb; 11 Mar; 15 Apr; 1 Jul; 26 Aug): Andrew Gwynne, Andrew Parnell, Anne Price, Annie Foot, Benjamin Palmer, Bob Minting, Caleb Palmer, Cameron Hutter (3), Caroline Rowe, Catherine Newman,

Chris Fuoco (2), Clare Melbourne, Dave Pateman, Dawn Walker, Derek Boustred, Di Hollidge (2), Dominic Harrower, Dylan Ravenscroft, Emily Brewer, Emma Scrace, Eve Pateman, Ezra Sullivan, Gary Evans, Gordon Seward (6), Helen Tailyour, Imogen Groves, Ivy-Mei Sullivan, Jackie Tordini, Jane Emma Pallanca, Jane Trollope, Jay Sweetman, Jemima Daly, Jenny Bjars, Joe Daly (3), John Fowler, John Gostling, John Kavanagh, John Ravenscroft, Jonathan Newman, Judy Ravenscroft (2), Julia Browne (2), Julie Finch, Katherine Gwynne, Katrina Vos, Keira Palmer, Kerry Nicola Richards, Les Turner (2), Lola Daly, Lucy Butt, Lucy Sizer (4), Lynda Garcia (3), Maggie Hunt, Mark Shaw (3), Martin Saxton (3), Mary Humphries, Mary Rowe (6), Meg Hepworth, Melanie Gostling, Mike Keep, Pat Clatworthy (3), Paul Keith Parker (2), Paul Palmer (2), Phil Penny (2), Philip Chivers (2), Philip Gater, Philippa Davies, Rhianna Greenslade, Richard Gentry, Roger Rowe (3), Roger Saunders, Sanad Twijiri, Sandie Reader (2), Sharon Greenslade, Sharon Vialls, Shaun Pickett, Simon Bunday (2), Siobhan Carnall, Sophie Butt, Steve Chapman (2), Steve Tordini, Sue Lewis (2), Sue Smye, Svetlana Johns, Tim Felton, Tim Landy, Tracey Cassidy (3), Tracey Hawker, Tracy Downs, Trudy Saxton, Vikki Thompson, Warren Killen (2), Wendy Land (2), Wilbur Sullivan, William Daly, Yasmin Jenner.

La Ramée, Toulouse (5 Aug; 12 Aug): Felix Alcock (2), Gregory Ewing, Jacqueline Alcock (2), Jason Raaum, Jérôme Costinot (2), Matt Ellis (2), Robyn Ellis (2).

Ludlow (13 May): Debbie Bean, Emma Tipton, Frank Luscott, Geoff Kinlen, Geoff Mutton, Gilly Pitt, Iain Prentice, Joseph Manley, Nikki Martin, Paul Baskeyfield, Paul Nolan, Peter Cartwright, Simon Dixon, Sue Manley, Tina Cartwright, Wendy Booker.

Parke (14 Jan; 4 Feb; 4 Mar; 8 Apr; 29 Apr; 29 Jul; 9 Sep; 23 Dec): Alison Hydon (5), Andrew Watson (3), Andy Hard, Angela Evans (5), Ann Pascoe, Annabelle Evans, Anne-Marie Baker (3), Charlie Churchill, Claire Ayling, Cliff Barnes (3), Craig Churchill, David Stokes, Deborah Sommerfeld, Doug Smith, Erica Ross, Ewan Walton (2), Finn Hearn, Gemma Radcliffe, Geoff Woods, Graham Neal (6), Jill Bishop, Jim Cromwell, John Cornish (7), Jon Murray, Joseph Arkle, Justine Sutton, Kathryn Steemson, Ken Dyer (4), Kieran Dore (7), Lauren Smart (4), Leo Brooke (3), Lucy Ayling, Martha Neal, Mary Cornish (3), Nick Moore, Oliver Mortimer (2), Owen Sutton, Philip Pike (2), Richard Golesworthy, Ro Cartwright, Rob Parkinson, Rob Pollard (2), Robert William Howe, Rosie Steemson, Sally Murray, Sally Shoolbraid (6), Steve Cain, Tamsin Cromwell, Tim Pratt (2), Tim Sleath (4), Wilfrid Taylor, Zilpah Walton.

Plym Valley (28 Jan; 24 Jun): Aimi Hewlett Elliott (2), Bryonie Taylor-Green, Carrie Laws, Charlie Tucker, Chloe Hoatson, Darren Hewlett (2), Dave Beckenkrager, Dave Connell, David Salvage, Eunice Halliday, Ffion Barham, Graham Bale, Jennifer McLarnon, Jessica Rich (2), Katie Boxall, Katy Mogridge (2), Leon Dawes, Lisa Alford, Lorna Domeney, Louise Rymel, Mary Frances Dyer, Matthew

Rich, Nina Hall (2), Paul Elliott, Russ Mogridge, Sarah Curtin, Sharon Adams, Sharon Beckenkrager, Stephen Boxall, Stephen Panton, Susan Rich, Tracey May.

Preston Park (22 Jul): Alexander George, Ali Guihen, Angelina Smy, April Williams, David Hoy, Eve Eley, Geraldine Moffat, Henry McLaughlin, Hugh Gosney, Joe Hemstedt, Jon Ridge, Jude Aldred, Lucy Anderson, Maria Pali, Michael Jarvis, Mo Touray, Nathalie Rouquet, Nick Hearn, Nicky Yeates, Paige Richardson, Rose Patricia Wilmot, Sarah Thomas, Steve Rooney, Terry James Avey, Tim Jukes.

Torbay Velopark (31 Dec 2016; 25 Feb; 25 Mar; 6 May; 15 Jul; 16 Sep; 14 Oct; 11 Nov): Alex Radcliffe (2), Alice Whitehead, Alison Ford (2), Amelia Baybutt, Amelia Bumby, Anabel Astle (2), Angus Glass, Anita Ley (2), Ann Gazzard (2), Antje Jaeger (2), Archie Thompson (2), Barbara Young, Ben Brugge, Brenda Grant (2), Brian Lewis, Bridget Williams (3), Callum Jeffery, Carol Peakman (2), Cassandra Harrison (5), Chad Nelson (3), Chris Reece (3), Claire Taylor, Dani Dodwell, Daniela Kutz, David Cubberley (2), Eileen Severn, Elizabeth (Lizzie) Bumby, Ellee-Mae Forkes (2), Emma Gilboy (3), Evalyn Flanagan, Fleur Ricklin, Gary Brenton (2), Gary Caunter, Gemma Radcliffe, George Oldridge (2), Hannah Carr, Howard Brugge, Huseyin Kemal, Ian Hayward (3), Ian Roblin (3), Jan Pryor, Jasper Harrison-Bayes (3), Jasper Wright, Jeremy Goddard (3), Jo Canham (3), Jo Coish (3), Jo Loten, Joanne Smith, John Drennan (4), John Francis (2), John Potter, Johnny Village, Julia Glass,

Julia Tysoe, Julyan Bayes (2), Karen Bumby, Karen Frissen, Karen Hill, Kate Maud, Kathryn Checkley (3), Katie Brooks (2), Katie Ford, Katie Kies, Keith Belt (2), Kerry Bell (4), Kirsten Mundy, Laura Kies, Lauren Carr, Liam Adams, Liz Sampson, Lotta Savola, Lucy Nelson, Lynne Gibson, Maddy Brugge, Maddy Dodwell, Malcolm Nelson, Marc Walpot, Mark Harding, Mark Hardy, Michelle Coles, Mike Parker, Nicholas Whitfield, Nick Robinson (3), Ole Dodwell, Oliver Oldridge (2), Paul Frissen, Paul Tout, Pauline Marr, Peter Davis, Roger Matthews (2), Samantha Froggatt (5), Sammy Ingham (2), Sara Jane Crozier (5), Sarah Addis (5), Shaun McKernan (6), Silbury Peakman, Simon Gilboy (6), Simon Toms, Stephen Lofthouse, Stephen Wilbraham (7), Steve Carr, Steve Hookins (2), Steve Maddock (2), Steve Wright, Stuart Batten (2), Tegan Reed-Gallimore (2), Tessa Ley, Tom Wright (2), Vince Langdon, Wilf Wright (4).

Thank you, one and all.

KEEP

ON

RUNNING

THE HIGHS
& LOWS OF A
MARATHON ADDICT

Phil
Hewitt

KEEP ON RUNNING

Phil Hewitt

ISBN: 978 1 84953 236 5

Paperback

£9.99

Marathons make you miserable, but they also give you the most unlikely and the most indescribable pleasures. It's a world that I love – a world unlocked when you dress up in lycra, put plasters on your nipples and run 26.2 miles in the company of upwards of 30,000 complete strangers.

Phil Hewitt, who has completed 30 marathons in conditions ranging from blistering heat to snow and ice, in locations round the globe from London to New York, sets a cracking pace in this story of an ordinary guy's addiction to marathon running. Reliving the highs and lows along the way, this light-hearted account of his adventures on the road examines the motivation that keeps you going when your body is crying out to stop. Above all, it tries to answer the ultimate question: 'Why do you do it?'

Have you enjoyed this book?

If so, why not write a review on your favourite website?

If you're interested in finding out more about our books,
find us on Facebook at **Summersdale Publishers** and follow
us on Twitter at **@Summersdale**.

Thanks very much for buying this Summersdale book.

www.summersdale.com